NEVER SING LOUDER THAN LOVELY

Never Sing Louder Than Lovely

ISOBEL BAILLIE

HUTCHINSON

London Melbourne Sydney Auckland Johannesburg

For Nancy
To fill in all the gaps while I was away from her

Hutchinson & Co. (Publishers) Ltd

An imprint of the Hutchinson Publishing Group

17–21 Conway Street, London W1P 6JD

Hutchinson Group (Australia) Pty Ltd
30–32 Cremorne Street, Richmond South, Victoria 3121
PO Box 151, Broadway, New South Wales 2007

Hutchinson Group (NZ) Ltd
32–34 View Road, PO Box 40–086, Glenfield, Auckland 10

Hutchinson Group (SA) (Pty) Ltd
PO Box 337, Bergvlei 2012, South Africa

First published 1982
Reprinted 1983 (twice)

© Isobel Baillie and Bryan Crimp 1982

Set in Bembo

Printed in Great Britain by The Anchor Press Ltd
and bound by Wm Brendon & Son Ltd
both of Tiptree, Essex

British Library Cataloguing in Publication Data
Baillie, Isobel
Never sing louder than lovely.
1. Baillie, Isobel   2. Singers—Great Britain
—Biography
I. Title
784'.092'4   ML420.B/
ISBN 0 09 150460 0

Contents

'The best of all trades is to make songs
And the second best is to sing them.'
HILAIRE BELLOC

List of Illustrations

Prologue

'Why don't you write a book?'

Over the years I have lost count of the number of times I have been asked this question. It might come from a young aspiring soprano who admires the dress I am wearing, who hears the applause and would like to emulate something similar, or it might herald from a 'fan' who wants to 'enquire within', to dig below the surface in order to discover what makes this particular singer 'tick'. The latter will certainly be disappointed if he expects to find a full and revealing portrait of my personal life as wife and mother; within these covers I have concerned myself primarily with the accumulated impressions and reminiscences of my career as a singer. That aspiring singer might discover something of use though I must emphasise that she will find no easy 'method', no key to instant success. I have also deliberately eschewed a blow-by-blow chronological account of what has proved a lengthy and, for me, eventful life, for nothing is surely more off-putting than a seemingly endless succession of places and dates and the accompanying vacuous paeans of praise. Instead I have attempted to present portraits and memories of the many musicians I have encountered during my years as a singer, simultaneously outlining the general pattern of my life.

I am a mere *singer* and the prospect of writing a book was a daunting if not terrifying prospect. During the years each request has consequently received an abrupt, automatic reaction: 'Never!' Eventually I was enticed by Bryan Crimp to commit myself to print. Without his assistance and encouragement this book would never have been written.

9

Perhaps I should explain the reason for my basic reluctance in putting pen to paper. Without wishing to appear falsely modest I have been unwilling to embark upon such a venture as I do not think my kind of career was important enough. When I read the autobiographies of today's 'superstars' and their resultant impact upon the world I feel I have far less excitement and glamour to offer. Yet I do know that as a singer I *was* different. Precious few singers of my generation entered the musical world as I did and certainly no singer today would be prepared to serve such an arduous, lengthy, yet what was for me supremely enjoyable apprenticeship. Also, unlike so many singers I did not seek publicity; if it came it came – and was welcome for I am as human as the next person – but I would never go out and, as the glossy magazines might put it, 'court fame'. My long life has, however, been a continuous joy which I hope the reader will be able both to savour and to share.

CHAPTER ONE

Beginnings

ALTHOUGH most people consider me to be a Mancunian I was born just north of the Border in Hawick; Scots by parentage, for both my parents were of Scottish descent, and Scots by birth. Hawick was therefore where I spent my earliest years though my memories of the town itself during the closing years of the nineteenth century are few, for I was far too young to absorb the images which surrounded me in that quiet, welcoming town. I do remember the River Tweed running through the centre of Hawick, but my only other memories of this time come from holidays spent just outside Hawick, after the family had moved to Newcastle-upon-Tyne; most indelibly the cottage on the estate of the Duke of Buccleuch where my paternal grandfather worked as a carpenter. His extraordinary fondness for working with wood spilt over into his precious spare time which would be spent fashioning violins and some exquisite fretwork clocks. Taken to Bowhill, the ducal estate, by my sisters, I would romp and revel in its open unbounded freedom. My grandfather's cottage stands to this day and when I revisited it some eighty years later I saw the same magnificent raspberries and the same 'Paddy's Well' nestling in the hillside. Why 'Paddy's Well', in Scotland of all places, I never knew but the water was exceptionally pure and fresh and is still frequently sampled by the present Duke.

I saw much less of my maternal grandfather Robert Douglas, a weaver. He lived in a little house in Selkirk and earned himself a considerable reputation in the local pubs on account of his dramatic recitations, particularly of Robert Burns. He was also passionately devoted to cricket and wrote a most knowledgeable

11

book about the game as played in the Border counties. Few humble weavers working within the confines of their cottage could surely boast of having written a book and had it published!

My father's pride in his ancestry was reflected in the family names bestowed upon his four children. His only son and first born was christened Alexander Dickson, the three subsequent daughters Margaret Hetherington, Ann Pott and, in 1895, the little after-thought, Isabella Douglas – a vague connection with the infamous Douglas clan no doubt! It was a pride I too inherited. For example, it was a particularly memorable day in 1942 when I was invited to become a patron of the Glasgow Border Counties Association. Other patrons numbered the Dukes of Buccleuch and Roxburghe while the President was none other than the Earl of Home. Eventually, it seems, we all instinctively return to our roots.

Father was a master baker who specialised in those Scots delights – pancakes, baps, scones and shortbread. As was traditional in those days, he used to rise at five o'clock in order that his customers would be sure of their hot baps for breakfast. His shortbread was quite special: never have I ever tasted anything which remotely approached my father's. The bakehouse was situated at the back of the house part way up a hill. Outside, always on view, was an enormous wooden barrel into which all the apple cores, the only remnants of father's equally famous apple tarts, would be thrown. With uncharacteristic bravado I would furtively make my way to the barrel and steal some of the cores, their taste heightened by the daring circumstances under which they were obtained and eaten.

Next to the bakehouse was the stable where the pony and trap were kept, our only means of transport which served not only to deliver father's products but also as the family conveyance. On special occasions we would be bundled into the trap and taken to Bowhill in order to visit my grandfather. My mother never tired of telling me how, on one such visit, the pony fell between the shafts of the cart and I, a mere babe, was catapulted out of the trap only to land between the horse's front legs. This could account for a lot in later life!

Father's empire expanded when we moved to Newcastle-upon-Tyne when I was about five years old. He was now responsible for three shops. It was during our comparatively brief stay here that my two sisters formed a close friendship with a school chum who sang. One day with great glee they announced that they were to hear her sing at a concert. In what was really my first ever encounter, admittedly a very indirect one, with 'a singer' I shared their bubbling excitement and envied them their outing. I, of course, was sent off to bed though there was something about the venture which deeply impressed me and prevented me from sleeping. On my sisters' return I lay silent and still, drinking in every word of their conversation which graphically conveyed to me the thrill of that concert. Not only did I discover that the friend had sung particularly well but that, according to Margaret, 'She even got an encore!' This puzzled me greatly and so I arose very early the next morning and made my way to the friend's house nearby. Naturally she was most surprised to find me on the doorstep alone and at such an early hour. 'Why Bella!', she exclaimed, 'What are you doing here so early?' 'Oh', I said, full of curious anticipation, 'I've come to see your encore!'

It was while we were living in Newcastle-upon-Tyne that I also experienced my first encounter with the moving pictures, in this instance Joan of Arc being burnt at the stake; strong fare for such a youngster. I was so moved I could not sleep for nights. It marked the beginning of a life-long fascination with the cinema. Whenever a travelling fair came to town I would invariably disappear, though no one in the family would worry unduly as I could always be located, mesmerised and transfixed in the moving picture tent. Perhaps such a love, plus a later addiction for the theatre, proved some kind of compensation for the fact that my chosen career took in very little of the acting side of singing.

It was not long before we moved yet again. Continuing our pilgrimage southwards the family moved to Manchester where my father now ran five shops, including one in Princess Road where I attended the Board school. However good he was as a baker, and despite the enlarging of his business, father was not a particularly successful manager of his affairs for there was rarely a great deal of money to be spent on the family. This is not to say, though, that we did not eat well – father, for example, always had cream in his tea, a weakness that, to this day, I continue to share. While these moves resulted in a building up of his business I think they arose from an innate restlessness which was part and parcel of his make-up.

Then, suddenly and quite unexpectedly, father died. The family soon found itself in very difficult circumstances. The precious profits of father's labours had naturally been ploughed back into the business and the shops had, of course, only been rented (in those days 'ordinary folk' were unable to buy property), so the businesses were shut down without remuneration. All, that is, with the exception of the shop in Moss Lane East which was valiantly taken on by my brother, then only fourteen. I even remember hauling around to the other bakers in the city a large hot plate which my father had used to make his Scotch pancakes. I could only have been eight or nine but eventually I triumphantly sold it for five pounds, a much needed boost to the family income. Fortunately mother was a brilliant manager and we never went hungry. She produced stews and shepherd's pies and, quite miraculously, made a quarter of tea last the family an entire week. Morning breakfast was *always* porridge.

It was solely owing to young Alex that the family was provided for until my sisters were able to go out to work, Margaret tackling office work and Ann braving the dry cleaning business, then very much in its infancy. Three years later, once Alex was sure that the family was set squarely back on its feet, he left home armed only with a supply of his own special brand of little hard bread rolls – even at that age my brother was a confirmed health addict, the then popular 'health man' Sandow being his idol. For years Alex had wanted to travel – some of my father's wanderlust had obviously rubbed off onto him – and now he grabbed his opportunity. Travelling steerage to America, he landed in New Orleans and worked his way across the continent by labouring on farms and such like before eventually ending up at Long Beach, California, where he took a job in a large hotel baking scones and baps for the afternoon teas. Always a meticulous person, like father before him he would get up at five, hours before his fellow workers, in order to get all his baking complete and his utensils cleaned by midday, thus enabling him to go off to the beach where he could undertake his daily reading. He was a compulsive reader; if his education had been curtailed because of having left school to maintain the family he more than compensated for such a loss by his extraordinarily wide-ranging literary taste. Yet his colleagues grew resentful of young Baillie slipping off at midday while they continued to labour until five or six o'clock at night and eventually the manager summoned Alex into his office to investigate the series of complaints which had been filed against him. My brother instantly took the initiative and asked if the complaints were in any way connected with his work. 'No', came the reply, 'Your work is splendid. It stems from the fact that you finish work each day at 12 o'clock.' 'Yes', said Alex, 'and I shall continue to go off at midday when my work is finished and if you don't like it I'll leave.' He might have been a youngster but he took his stand and made his point, something he did thoughout his life, such was his positive nature.

A while later he married Marie, the daughter of a lady doctor. His utterly charming wife did, however, have a permanent complaint, the garden always appeared to be exceptionally dirty underfoot. There appeared to be no escape, no remedy from this insidious dirt which was forever being trodden into the carpets and which infiltrated every corner of the house. Eventually they left, selling the house for a modest sum only to discover just a little later that the 'dirt' had been oil and the land was worth a fortune. Not long afterwards Alex jumped ship to Honolulu and was put to work in the galley. Again he so impressed everyone with his many skills that they tried to persuade him to stay on. But this was not part of his plan. Within a short while of settling in Honolulu he arranged for Marie to join him and had opened a gramophone shop. Inspired by the products he sold Alex was soon making the first ever recordings of Hawaian music. Honolulu remained his home for the rest of his life and his house became a welcoming and enjoyable refuge during my subsequent travels.

But it was intended that this chapter should be devoted to my early years and I must therefore once again return to the beginning of this century. The family's earliest recollection of my singing was when my sisters took me to a Sunday School party. At some stage in the proceedings they apparently stood me on a table where I sang *All things bright and beautiful* to those who cared to listen. I was about five at the time. It was, of course, the era of home entertainment, including singing around the piano, and my impromptu recital consequently did not appear at all exceptional. By the time we had moved to Manchester I apparently was always singing around the house, to such an extent that it prompted my father, not long before his death, to remark to my mother, 'Biddy, you know, there is "something" about Bella's voice which is different!' But we *all* sang. Mother had a fine voice – I learnt many Scottish folk tunes at her knee – while both my sisters were musical and sang in the local church choir. I was also informed that my brother when a small lad possessed a splendid treble voice. He even once played the principal role in a Hawick presentation of *Francis Osbaldeston*, a popular musical work of the time.

Although I sang almost from the cradle my voice was not 'discovered' until I was about nine years old when it was heard by the headmaster of my Board school, T. H. Bramwell. It was the custom to assemble the entire school on a Friday afternoon for a final communal sing-song period. The music chosen generally included some well-loved hymns, enabling everyone to participate. I can still remember the day when my teacher, Miss South, whispered something to the headmaster and he requested that I sing the second verse of *The day thou gavest* as a solo. I was neither frightened nor nervous for singing was already as natural and inevitable to me as breathing and eating. Nothing was said at the time but the following week Mr Bramwell sent for me and taught me a song by Hope Temple called *An old garden*. A little later I took part in a school pageant, a true Empire Day extravaganza, called *Britannia*. All the colonies were represented by their varied costumes and I played Britannia singing something suitably patriotic. Mr Bramwell continued to teach me various different songs: my ear was sharp and receptive though at that time I knew nothing of notes or note values. His special interest in my voice was to last long after I left the care and concern of his school.

From the Board school I won a scholarship to the High School in Dover Street, now the Manchester High School. Most of the pupils were fee paying and rarely lost an opportunity to remind us scholarship girls of their 'superiority'. I well remember remarks being passed about my clothing as my mother was unable to afford the proper uniform. Nevertheless it proved to be a happy period of my life. Without wishing to boast I would say I was possibly above average in most subjects, enjoying in particular geography and history, though I was something of a duffer when it came to mathematics. Music played such an insignificant role at the High School that when I was summoned to the Headmistress's office for her to enquire about what job I had in mind before venturing into the outside world, I surprised her with my reply. With the utmost confidence I declared that I was going to be a singer. She smiled indulgently and exclaimed, 'Well yes dear, that's very nice as a hobby but I don't think you'll ever make a living at it!' Wrong as she was in this instance she was at all other times a wonderful and kind person.

My first job was in a music shop called Howards in Fountain Street. At the age of fifteen I was put in charge of the piano roll department, a splendid beginning to my contact with the outside world. Not that it had any particular influence upon me concerning musical matters but it was nevertheless most pleasing to be in a musical environment. There was also a gramophone department and I could listen to such tunes as *In the shadows* and other popular hits of the day. I frequently played piano rolls for my own pleasure, broadening my musical horizons even if they were not exactly my kind of music! The piano rolls were stored by number on shelves ranged around the entire department and the customers would consult a bulky catalogue before making their selection, not a great deal different from choosing a record today. For my labours I was paid eight shillings a week and walked three miles twice a day home and back, fair weather or foul. Mr Howard, the proprietor, once even asked me to sing at his church in Romiley, though this proved the only time he ever used my voice. This must have been one of my very earliest 'engagements', yet nearly seventy years later I received a letter from Mr Howard's then housekeeper who mentioned that she still vividly remembered that concert.

I think my very first ever professional engagement took place in a large church in Greenheys, Manchester. On the completion of my brief programme a gentleman kindly presented me with seven whole shillings and sixpence. My mother, who was with me, for I was still very young, walked me home via the grocer's where we bought some bacon as a special treat. My first fee had been sensibly employed!

But hiring out and dusting piano rolls, despite the musical connection, was not really for me. I consequently took an improving step and became a clerk in the gas department of the Manchester Town Hall! Once again I was as thrifty as I could be and frequently walked into town every day in order to save a penny bus fare. All this time Mr Bramwell maintained his interest in my voice and as I was now of the age when I could properly benefit from vocal lessons he persuaded my mother to allow me to commence serious studies.

And so I began tuition with Madam Jean Sadler-Fogg, the linch-pin of what was at that time Manchester's most musical family. Madam Sadler-Fogg was then still singing in a few concerts (I even performed with her at a church in Newton Heath in Manchester, singing second soprano to her principal line in *I waited for the Lord*) but she had more or less phased out her singing in favour of teaching. That she was a lyric rather than a dramatic soprano is reflected both in the manner and the works she taught me. She was a pupil of both Blanche Marchesi and William Shakespeare. Once she even took me to the legendary Marchesi who expressed a wish to hear my singing, though the only recollection I have of this awesome occasion was Marchesi's pronouncement: 'That F could be better!' I learnt Shakespeare's method of breathing. It always stood me in great stead and if ever I experienced doubts about any aspects of my singing I would always go back to my breathing. If that was right everything else appeared to fall naturally into place.

Studies with Madam Sadler-Fogg consisted of a single weekly lesson. Every lesson would consist of exercises: on vowels, consonants, scales, arpeggios and the like. I was, of course, in no way aware either of her aims or the ideas behind such exercises, and was merely content to comply with her wishes. Yet, like all eager pupils, I did not especially relish the exercises, being too keen to get on with the 'real singing', yet it was three long months before I was even allowed to sing a song. Once launched upon my career I continued, like so many singers who have found a teacher in whom they trust and have confidence, to grasp the occasional lesson with her until her death.

During those early days I was quite unable to pay her fees but once I had started to earn money from my engagements I attempted to make amends. I would hand over a sum at the end of each season, whatever I could afford. It was never a great deal but she appreciated the gesture. I was, and still remain all these years later, eternally grateful. I think Madam Sadler-Fogg realised that I had a talent and that the regular (and fortunately good) reports she heard concerning my early concerts in and around the Manchester area were more than adequate recompense.

After Madam Sadler-Fogg's death I continued to receive the occasional lesson from her husband Charles who taught me a great deal about singing with an orchestra. He was a true all-rounder and far from being 'just the Hallé organist'. Their son, Eric, was at this time branching out into modern music and it was he who taught me to tackle contemporary works. I consider myself to have been exceptionally fortunate in having made the acquaintance of such a musical family and I owe them an inestimable debt.

It was Charles Fogg who provided me with my first major local engagement. Organist of a church in Crumpsall near Manchester which regularly held concerts, Charles was responsible for my receiving an invitation to sing there and from that time onwards I was never short of engagements. Soon I was making as many as five appearances a week. This was how I managed to chalk up my first *Messiah* at the age of fifteen. My fee at this time never exceeded five pounds and more often than not averaged two or three guineas. At times, for very definite reasons still unknown to me, it was less; Madam Sadler-Fogg once secured an engagement for me at Waterfoot Church in the Rossendale Valley, advising me via a postcard that all had been arranged including the fee, most precisely noted in one corner as 'one and a half guineas'! Even that sum was worthy of consideration in those far off days.

Naturally these early engagements were confined to the immediate vicinity of Manchester, generally in church halls with small local choral societies and amateur orchestras. A broader spectrum of humanity could, however, be discovered in the halls of the then flourishing Cooperative Society where I also sang, though I obtained the biggest thrills from appearances in such venues as the city's Albert and Central Halls. The majority of these concerts would be devoted to ballads, ranging from such established and popular favourites as *Do you believe in fairies?* to the newer confections of Eric Coates and Haydn Wood, though occasionally, if an orchestra and choir were to hand, there would be a performance of an imposing smaller-scale work such as Mendelssohn's *Hymn of Praise*. Church performances concentrated largely upon oratorio which was very much part of musical life at that time. Practically every Anglican and Non-conformist church of any size would give an annual rendition of *Messiah* and in the larger churches this would be supplemented by additional performances of sacred works by Handel and Mendelssohn. These churches were also responsible for the annual musical weekends, the zenith of local musical life. These weekends usually consisted of an inaugural concert on the Saturday night, the performance of a complete oratorio during Sunday afternoon and a final concert, devoted exclusively to sacred music, on Sunday evening.

19

The church would be packed to the doors for every event. It frequently proved a considerable marathon for the poor singer but a highly enjoyable one. Two singers from London were normally engaged to participate with the rest of the team made up of local recruits. I became such a recruit, willing and, I hope, able to do my best.

Rather like the ripples caused by the throwing of a stone into a pond, so my appearances grew more numerous and spread further afield. Via word of mouth, the circles widened from Manchester to Bolton, Colne and Bacup, to Preston and Lancaster and then over the border to such Yorkshire strongholds as Bradford and Sheffield. Although I was still only in my teens I was never chaperoned. I would venture off on my own travelling by both bus and train and frequently returning very late at night. Such exploits do not bear thinking about today, yet at that time my mother found no cause to worry unduly, while I fearlessly considered myself to be a capable young thing! But after all, the world was then a much safer place than it is now.

CHAPTER TWO

Engagements

IT WAS at one of these local concerts in a small hall at Levenshume in Manchester that I first met my husband Harry. Henry Leonard Wrigley was a handsome, dashing young man with a considerable reputation as an entertainer. His speciality was recitations including, of course, *The green eye of the little yellow god*. I recall standing at the side of the stage watching him perform as I awaited my turn to sing with a feeling that amounted to something far more than simple admiration. Incredible as it might now appear I decided there and then that this was the man who would be my husband. I was just sixteen and to this day cannot explain such a precocious and totally uncharacteristic action.

During the ensuing months we frequently appeared at other concerts and consequently grew to know one another with unforced ease. Naturally there was no question of an immediate marriage; like most couples at this time we participated in the customary 'courtship'. It was to last seven years and ended on the last day of 1917 when we were married in St James's Church in Princess Road, just opposite my Board school, while Harry was home from the First World War on sick leave. He had contracted trench feet and at one stage there was even the dreaded shadow of amputation but Harry, strong and resilient, made a remarkable recovery – so much so that just two days after our marriage he was off to rejoin his regiment at the Front. I did not see him again until he returned wounded from the Battle of Ypres suffering from severe shrapnel wounds in the face. I later learnt he almost bled to death being carried across some four miles of duck-boarding to the nearest first-aid post.

Harry's wounds eventually healed and once more he returned to the battle though fortunately it was not long before the war came to its exhausted conclusion. Even so he did not return for he was placed in charge of a prisoner-of-war camp at Ypres. I still have a photograph of him riding high on horseback supervising the camp activities looking every inch a man in command. Despite his natural charm and easy humour Harry was a strict disciplinarian. Perhaps because of this the prisoners knew exactly where they stood with him and he was consequently well-liked. Indeed, when the camp was eventually disbanded the prisoners presented him with two large brass shell cases which they had exquisitely decorated with the barest of implements, a hammer and nail. He also returned with a bronze statuette of Joan of Arc which he had stumbled upon in the shattered remnants of Ypres.

Harry entered the war as a private in the Rifle Brigade whose headquarters were in Winchester. (Well over thirty years later after yet another world holocaust when Harry accompanied me to Winchester Cathedral, where I was due to sing, he was deeply moved to discover the pages of the Book of Remembrance open at the names of some of his closest friends.) As the war ground mercilessly on Harry took a commission and was consequently transferred to the Northumberland Fusiliers. When he finally returned to England after years of absence, it was as Major Wrigley. But there was no glory. He quickly discovered that the promised job 'which would be awaiting all loyal recruits' simply did not exist. And there was no pension or compensation.

Before the war Harry had worked in the cotton industry and so he naturally wished to return to the trade he knew. It proved particularly difficult. He was at a decided disadvantage in being one of the last to return home when all the vacancies had been well and truly filled. Fortunately we managed to survive on my earnings which not only supported Harry and me but also our daughter Nancy, born in December 1918 while Harry was at the Front, and my mother, who proved invaluable as baby-sitter, nurse, deputy mother and adoring grandmother. Harry eventually found a small niche in the cotton trade, though the overheads and expense of running an office in the centre of Manchester meant that there was little left at the end of the week. But he was happy to be busy and involved again and made his contribution to the maintenance of the household as and when he could.

It became obvious, however, that Harry would never completely recover from his injuries and his experiences at the Front. He was forced to lead life at a far more considered, measured pace. He never actively participated in my career assuming the role of doughty husband–manager as did so many husbands, but preferred to remain in the background attempting to make my life at home as easy as he could. When, for example, I returned home from an engagement he would meet me at the station with the car and have a meal prepared. Occasionally, mostly during the earlier years of our marriage, he would act as my chauffeur, a role which caused serious misunderstandings on more than one occasion. Once, for instance, Harry decided to drive me to one of my earliest regular 'haunts', the Rossendale Valley, where I was to sing at their annual musical weekend. After the Saturday morning rehearsal Harry took me to the house where I was to be given hospitality for the weekend. While I went to the front door Harry parked the car nearby. A dear old lady ushered me in with considerable warmth and kindness. The table, laid for high tea, groaned under the weight of every conceivable type of bread and cake – however anyone could be expected to sing after such a meal I would never know. After a while Harry came to the house and stood at the entrance to the living room where I was warming myself at the fire and talking to my hostess. Harry waited for a pause in the conversation in order that he might make himself known. The old lady observed all but kept talking having decided that Harry could, for some reason, wait a little longer. I discovered the reason for her attitude when, in the loudest stage whisper I have ever heard, she enquired, 'Will your chauffeur have his tea in't kitchen?' My 'chauffeur', never a shy creature at the best of times, was quick to reply, 'Ee, I'll be sleeping with her tonight!' After her initial shock the old lady grasped the situation and before the weekend was over she had become acquainted with the general drift of Harry's humour.

Harry was also taken for my chauffeur on another occasion at Glossop, near Stockport. It was a lovely May day when we arrived at the church where I was due to sing a recital. Harry dropped me at the church gates deciding that once he had parked the car he would take the air during my rehearsal. The church caretaker had viewed our arrival from afar and only approached Harry once I was safely inside. 'She's well known round these parts isn't she?' he ventured. Harry smiled and nodded his agreement, 'Oh yes, she's done a great deal of singing here for many years'. The caretaker, obviously seeing an opportunity for further conversation, pressed for further details, 'How old will she be then?' My husband politely informed him that I had reached the ripe old age of twenty-eight. 'Ah', said the caretaker with a knowing look adorning his face, 'She'll nown be a bad'n to work for!'

Harry sadly missed Nancy's formative years which seemed to pass so quickly. Before I knew it the local junior school was history and Nancy, now almost a young lady, was entering Withington High School. Here she revealed a flair for dramatics – could this have resulted from my obsession with the theatre and cinema? – but her head was most firmly fixed on the right way and she made no attempt at an artistic career, preferring instead to enter business college where she could learn a 'proper' trade. Naturally, I wondered whether she might turn to music and arranged for her to have piano lessons but the instrument did not appear to lie easily under her fingers. As I was anxious for her not to lose her love of music I did not press the matter. Singing was also not for her; she had a high soprano voice which seemed to start where mine left off – but she just did not want to be a singer. What she had and still possesses in abundance was a tremendous love for music and is today so highly informed about all that is going on in the music world that I can only silently admire.

It was, I think, shortly after the birth of Nancy that I began to realise just how foolish it was to be working in two opposing directions: my main job occupying most of my time with only evenings and weekends left to do what I loved best – singing. One night on my way home I treated myself to a tram ride, took out a postcard from my handbag and listed my earnings as a singer. They exceeded the salary I received from the Town Hall. I consequently made an instant and irrevocable decision: from that moment on I would devote all my time to singing.

Naturally my burning ambition was to sing with a large professional orchestra, an orchestra such as the Hallé whose concerts I regularly attended. I had long thrived on the memories of my first Hallé concert in which there were vocal soloists; although I remember neither the work nor all the soloists I do vividly recall the soprano, Florence Austral, regally dressed in a dark green gown and red slippers. So vivid was the impression she made upon me that I could only think of singing with such an orchestra and in such a hall. I consequently grasped the nettle and wrote to Hamilton Harty telling him of all that I had done and asking if he could give me an audition.

CHAPTER THREE

Hamilton Harty

ALTHOUGH Hamilton Harty is now best remembered as one of the greatest conductors to have graced these shores it was as an exceptionally gifted accompanist that he first made his mark when he arrived in London from his native Ireland at the turn-of-the-century. Shortly after his appointment as permanent conductor of the Hallé Orchestra in 1920 it became readily apparent that here was a very considerable force to be reckoned with. Also at this time, by dint of endless local engagements, I had become a familiar figure in and about Manchester though I still awaited a major break-through. It was therefore natural that I should look towards the Hallé and the commanding presence of Hamilton Harty, hence my decision to write informing him of all that I had done and asking if he could possibly hear me sing.

It was not long before I was seated in his office where I more or less reiterated the contents of my letter, stressing the fact that not only had I sung such sacred works as *Messiah*, *The Creation* and *Judas Maccabaeus* but that my repertoire even extended to operatic arias! All the while Harty listened kindly and attentively. Eventually he wound up the interview by saying that he would see what he could do, indicating that something might come along which he could offer me, and began to escort me to the door. I was crestfallen and only just managed to exclaim, 'But Mr Harty, you haven't heard me sing!' 'Oh yes I have', came the gentle, laughing reply. I was dumbfounded. He had, it transpired, slipped into the back of the Houldsworth Hall in Manchester during a midday concert devoted to the songs of Eric Fogg, the son of my teacher but, more importantly in this instance, the son of the Hallé organist – such was Harty's interest in his players. I, of course, was simply a willing guinea-pig, specially learning Eric's splendid little pieces for the occasion. Although Harty had come specifically to hear the work of the local young composer he obviously remembered my singing. Just three weeks after that interview I received a piece of manuscript through the post with his invitation to sing this work at a forthcoming Hallé concert.

It was the barcarolle, *The convent on the water*, from Alfredo Casella's symphonic suite *The Venetian Convent*, a movement containing a wordless soprano part which at that time appeared to my ears very avant-garde owing to its complex intervals and clustered chromaticisms. Harty had long displayed an interest in contemporary Italian music though he was not, I think, overimpressed by the musical content of this work. The suite contained music rescued by the composer from his ballet of the same name written for and rejected by Diaghilev. Casella also later admitted in his autobiography *Music in my Time* that *The Venetian Convent* was not one of his 'happier' works.

But there I was with a copy of this strange music staring me in the face. 'Well, here it is', I thought, 'I'll just have to learn it.' I went to the rehearsal totally confident that I knew every note of a very challenging manuscript. It was a confidence which instantly evaporated when I discovered that I had to sing from the back of the stage of the Free Trade Hall, some thirty yards or so from the conductor. All hopes of receiving some reassuring guidance from a position close to the conductor were totally dashed. So, from my eyrie near the organ console I joined the orchestral players and furiously counted the bars. Thus I made my Hallé début on 17 November 1921. Later that night I was due to sing at a banquet held in the Midland Hotel just a few yards away from the Free Trade Hall. As Harry escorted me to the hotel he remained ominously mute; obviously my first Hallé concert was to be my last. My feelings were confirmed when to my question 'Well, what was it like?', came the reply, 'Oh, it was *awful!*' I entered the hotel with a very heavy heart but who should enter the lift with us but Hamilton Harty who, at that time, was living at the Midland. He came forward, congratulated me, and informed me that it would not be long before he could give me something really rewarding to do from a singer's point of view.

Of these conflicting opinions it was Hamilton Harty's which, fortunately for me, was supported in the next day's press. Samuel

Langford, the highly respected *Manchester Guardian* critic, wrote: 'Mme Bella Baillie is greatly to be congratulated on giving the difficult chromatic vocalisation in the barcarolle with such clarity and effect and purity of intonation.' I also remember the concert for another reason. The great Casals was the soloist in Schumann's Cello Concerto and he autographed a score for me: 'To Miss Bella Baillie with my congratulations for her beautiful singing, Pablo Casals', which meant even more than the favourable review in the *Manchester Guardian*. Hamilton Harty remained true to his promise concerning further and more rewarding work with the Hallé and only a short while after that Casella performance he gave me a *Creation* and what proved to be the very first BBC broadcast of *Messiah*.

A few years later Harty advised me to make an adjustment to my name. Up to that time I had used 'Bella Baillie', the name by which I was known to everyone, but he felt that it led one to expect a music hall or musical comedy artist. The alliteration enabled the name to roll a little too easily off the tongue. Needless to say the subject was broached with typical tact and kindness:

Dear Bella,

A rather delicate matter! I have been so annoyed lately at the refusal of certain people to engage you that I have asked them straight out what is wrong. In each case they have answered that they don't think your name, itself, is striking enough for advertisement purposes. One said, 'If only she were Isabel Baillie it would be so different.' Don't be annoyed – I believe they are right and I want you to think seriously of adopting this style in future.

The only reason I have for writing this is a wish to help you. I'm sure you will understand this.

Yours sincerely,
Hamilton Harty

His concern was genuine and sincere. I did not particularly relish the idea of changing my name but I acquiesced; as with just about everything he did Harty was, of course, absolutely right, though naturally the adjustment took some getting used to on both sides. To this day there are still some very old friends in Manchester who call me Bella.

Harty's advice was ever ready but given only when required and then with considerable kindness and insight. It was, for ex-

28

ample, Sir Hamilton who instilled into me that vocal colour can arise from one's thoughts as one sings. Serious consideration of the text automatically colours the voice, as do mental images, possibly the most common way of creating vocal colour. For example, in the recitative *There were shepherds abiding in the fields* from Part 1 of *Messiah* I would conjure up in my mind a dark blue sky and the feel of that chill night air. Such a mental picture creates a mood which in turn colours the voice.

Only once in 1928 when the BBC asked if I would participate in a Wagner broadcast did I incur Harty's displeasure. Up to that time I had sung what I can only describe as 'light Wagner', *Elsa's dream* from *Lohengrin* for example, as I felt I was not entirely suited either vocally or temperamentally for Wagner. Yet the thrill of singing against the rich orchestral backcloth of Wagner's scores was most difficult to resist. After serious thought I decided to accept the invitation despite the dangers. My decision was based on the knowledge that as I would be singing into a studio microphone my voice would not have to be unduly strained as the balance with the orchestra could be achieved by mechanical means. Imagine my consternation when, a few days after the broadcast, I received the following:

Dear Bella,

I see, by accident, that you have been singing such things as the closing scene from *The Ring* – I believe you know in your heart that this is not wise. Your voice is too lyrical and fresh for this kind of heavy-weight work.

You will know that I am only writing in this way because I wish for your real success. I have really no business to interfere with what you consider right to do – but you know how straightforward I am about music. I have been glad to do what little I could to help forward your charming talent but if you feel you must continue to sing music which cannot possibly suit your voice and personality then I must retire just wishing you whatever good luck remains for you in your musical life.

I am really disappointed in you, Bella, I thought you had enough sense to see that in your own line you have most of the sopranos beaten – but in music of the type I refer to you are quite out of the picture and merely a source of gratification to your enemies. Don't be cross, I really believe what I am saying.

Yours ever sincerely,
Hamilton Harty

Naturally I replied though I now do not remember in what vein. It must have been in agreement with him as it prompted this conciliatory olive branch:

Dear Bella,

As I someway expected, you have been good and sensible enough not to take my scolding the wrong way. It is not exactly *I* who have any right to feel displeasure but the decent ideals of music to which we *still* all cling are the only things worth while considering in our art. When you die I want someone to write on your grave, 'She was a sweet singer who always respected music' – not 'She made £10,000 by prostituting her pure and fresh talent.'

Well, that's all right again. I am soon returning to Manchester and, of course, I shall be glad to resume our peculiar lessons. Bella, in your professional work always try to take a long view. If you are hard up for money you can have mine – what I've got – but for goodness sake keep the one thing that makes you a little different to millions of others unspoiled and good enough to be delivered back to whoever it came from originally. (Isn't he a fine preacher!)

That's all. Love and friendship and a brotherly embrace.

Yours sincerely,
Hamilton Harty

This episode taught me one of the most useful lessons of my life: respect for one's own voice. A singer should never attempt roles which tax the voice.

Such was Harty's forgiveness that he later took me to Bradford specifically to sing a Wagner programme! (I also once surprised him when I took part in a performance of the Quintet from *Die Meistersinger* in a Hallé concert; coming off stage he remarked *sotto voce* that he had just discovered that I could 'bawl like any operatic soprano!') A strange incident connected with that Bradford Wagner concert occurred some thirty years or so later when I was singing in a little church in the West Country. A Mr Behrens, a member of that famous Manchester family who have long been loyal and devoted supporters of the Hallé Orchestra, came around to the vestry after the recital clutching the actual Bradford programme and saying 'Miss Baillie, I want you to see this. It's the one and only time in my life I ever heard *all* the words!' A kind personal tribute but also a remarkable judgement on the quality of Harty's orchestral accompaniments. He was

30

indeed the most sympathetic accompanist a singer could wish for; whether at the piano or with an orchestra he appeared to breathe with you.

Hamilton Harty took a personal interest in every member of his orchestra and knew exactly what they could and could not play. I have seen him take endless pains with an oboist or horn player in order to get a passage just as he wanted, yet it was always done in the most friendly manner. Not once did I ever hear him shout at an orchestra. He was an exceptionally quiet man with the most beautiful speaking voice; truly a gentle genius. His remarkable personal relationship with his orchestra paid handsome dividends for he was worshipped by his players, and under his direction the Hallé reached its highest ever achievements. It not only became, for most of us, the finest orchestra in the country but ranked among the very best in Europe. Harty's programmes were always refreshing and challenging; long before it became fashionable I remember him presenting programmes comprising three great symphonies, something unheard of in those days. He also served contemporary music, particularly the kind that could boast a melody! With the Hallé he gave the British premières of Mahler's Ninth Symphony (1930) and Shostakovich's First Symphony (1932) and in 1929 he was the stunning pianist in the world première of Lambert's *Rio grande*. With the BBC Symphony Orchestra he introduced Walton's First Symphony to an astonished world in 1935.

Harty could also be a difficult person for, despite his gentleness, he was capable of being exceptionally firm and holding strong, positive beliefs. He once, for example, told me that he had been asked to consider a high-powered position at the BBC but had refused as he could not have endured the inevitable bureaucracy. It nearly broke his heart when, in 1930, he lost so many of his finest players to the newly formed BBC Symphony Orchestra and again, just a few years later, when he lost more members to a northern BBC orchestra. This must have been one of the prime contributory factors to his resignation from the Hallé in 1933. It is all so very different nowadays when conductors travel all over the world, with so few truly attached to one orchestra and never 'knowing' their orchestra as did Harty.

To appreciate him at his greatest as a conductor he had to be heard playing Berlioz. I learnt the whole of *The Trojans at Carthage* with him as an understudy when he was preparing for a rare UK

31

performance in 1929. Alas, the imported soprano did not fall ill so I never did get a chance of singing *The Trojans* with Harty – but what an experience that concentrated period of study proved. He once told me that he felt an instinctive affinity with Berlioz, something proven by his performances.

Harty's humour was gentle, occasionally mischievous and very quick, a point readily demonstrated by the now legendary story of Artur Schnabel's first visit to the Hallé in 1930. After a non-chalant, cigar-puffing start to the rehearsal of Brahms's First Piano Concerto Schnabel soon realised that the Hallé ought to be taken seriously; the resultant concert was superb with the single exception that Schnabel omitted two bars in the finale. Harty, the supreme orchestral accompanist, remained quite unruffled and gave an instant cue: the entire orchestra corporately jumped two bars. Afterwards Harty and Schnabel discussed the performance with the then leader of the orchestra, Alfred Barker. 'Hmm! Bravo, bravo!' said the obviously impressed pianist, which prompted Harty to enquire, somewhat roguishly, 'As good as the Berlin Philharmonic?' Schnabel hesitated somewhat, 'Oh, do you think so?' 'Yes,' said Harty emphatically, 'Two bars better!' Schnabel returned to the Hallé the following season to play Brahms's Second Piano Concerto.

I sang many of Harty's compositions, all of which revealed a quite remarkable understanding of the human voice. One of the most magical of all is his setting of Keats's *Ode to a nightingale*, given its première by his wife Agnes Nicholls in 1907. It requires the singer's full range of vocal colour from the *pianissimo* opening stanza:

> My heart aches, and a drowsy numbness pains
> My sense, as though of hemlock I had drunk

to the thrilling climactic section:

> Away! Away! for I will fly with thee,
> Not charioted by Bacchus and his pards.

Possibly my most memorable Harty performance was the première of his *The Children of Lir* given under his baton on 1 March 1939 in the Queen's Hall, London. A most compelling work based upon an Irish legend it depicts, in the composer's own words:

> the four children of King Lir changed into white swans and

doomed to wander over the Irish waters for a thousand years. So for this long time did these four swans haunt the lakes and seas of Ireland, at the end coming to the sea of Moyle, which is the tempestuous stretch of water between the Irish and Scottish coasts. One morning as they swam off the wild and rugged cliffs of Antrim, the swan-children suddenly heard the sound of a bell from a little church on the cliff top. Immediately they were changed back into their human shapes, noble and beautiful still, but incredibly old. They were taken by the coast people to the little church and baptised, and as they were received into the Christian faith they died.

It is a highly rhapsodic work with a vocalise-type role for soprano solo representing the singing of Finola, the only girl among the children of Lir. The work's exceptional depths appear to stem from a deep personal cry from the heart. Once again I was placed at the back of the stage near the organ so that my voice carried over the top of the orchestra. Did 'Hay', as Harty was affectionately known to his closest friends, remember the effect from my Hallé début with him eighteen years earlier? I never knew. This première of *The Children of Lir* sadly proved to be my last concert with him as his health began to fail rapidly.

Hamilton Harty was not only responsible for launching my professional career in my 'home territory', he also suggested that I should temporarily desert my family and friends for vocal studies in Italy. It took me a while to summon up enough courage to take what was at that time a momentous step, for I had no financial means to enable me to undertake such a course of action. Harty, well aware of my plight, gently implied that if such an idea involved financial difficulties something could most surely be done – I think he had in mind the raising of a bursary as he had many influential friends who took a keen interest in singing and who would have undoubtedly been prepared to sponsor a young singer. But I was proud, possibly too much so considering the effort and strain these studies were to involve, and told him that I was, naturally, immensely grateful but that I would be able to manage quite well. I think it was in the summer of 1925 that I went off to Italy, alone and full of trepidation though securing a degree of comfort in the knowledge that Nancy would be happy and contented with my mother. We all managed to survive somehow on the fees of my engagements from the preceding months. At that time the London season lasted from September, comm-

encing with the Proms, and concluded in May, so I earned as
much as I could during that season, frantically saving in order to
pay for my own travel, fees and keep, as well as ensuring the
maintenance of the rest of the family.

Hamilton Harty recommended that I should approach Gug-
lielmo Somma, a remarkably fine vocal coach and now possibly
best remembered as tutor and mentor to one of Italy's greatest
baritones, Riccardo Stracciari; at this time he also held an advisory
position with the Italian branch of the Gramophone Company.
Before I left Harty repeatedly emphasised that Somma would not
be giving me a voice but that he would most certainly teach me
'the tricks of the trade'. Somma, then a man in late middle-age,
taught in a quiet restrained manner, the very antithesis of so many
of today's teachers who are inclined to equate decibels with mus-
icality. But perhaps I should have expected such an approach for
wasn't Harty the quietest and gentlest of people? They were
obviously kindred spirits. Somma made no attempt to enlarge
my voice, opting instead to achieve an evenness of tone throughout its entire range. Somma's efforts were, it appeared to some
ears, successful; Sir George Dyson, for example, used to say that
for him the chief attraction of my voice was its evenness from
top to bottom.

For two hard-working but invigorating summers I had a daily
lesson with Maestro Somma, sometimes as early as eight o'clock
in the morning. Until I had conquered the Italian language all
lessons were conducted in French as Somma spoke very little
English. I lived in a little top floor pensione opposite the Duomo
in Milan though I ate with all the many other girls who seemed
to surround me on all sides. Everyone was exceptionally friendly
and it was some considerable time before I discovered that the
entire area was *libero ingresso*! I had put down the many advances
I had received to that innate forwardness characteristic of the
Italian male. Will I, for example, ever forget the attentions of a
bronzed, good-looking soldier who approached me one balmy
evening as I came down the stairs and politely asked where I was
going? 'Alla cinema,' I proclaimed with quiet determination.
'Sola?' he asked in amazement. 'Sì,' I replied resolutely, 'Sola!'
(Even in Italy and with such limited financial means I still
attempted to keep abreast of films even if it did mean changing
one's seat many times!) But Italy would not, of course, be Italy
if one did not have to endure the constant pinching, a striking

contrast to being asked to leave Milan cathedral because I was wearing a short-sleeved dress.

After my daily lesson I would practise. I was fortunate enough to have a piano squeezed into my room so that I could prepare for the next day's lesson. Although I was no pianist as such – I would have loved to have played well and still regret not having been able to further my childhood studies – I was competent enough to teach myself all the repertoire which confronted me. Working with Somma proved a joy even if he was meticulous in his demands. I arranged that he assist me with the repertoire planned for the forthcoming Prom season. With one such song, Schubert's *Shepherd on the rock*, it seemed that I was quite unable to sing the first phrase in a way that even approached pleasing my exacting teacher. He continually heard something in the third note which displeased him and went over the offending phrase time and time again. Eventually the trouble was located: it was the way I sang the word 'on' of the opening phrase 'T'was on the highest rock'. I was singing in English and the vowel sound was one which Somma was just not used to.

My studies in Italy taught me many things, some of which might be considered to be of minor importance, though they were to stand me in good stead for the rest of my life. Most importantly I learnt to listen to myself and to pitch a note mentally before it was sung: both absolutely essential for accurate intonation. I also discovered the correct employment of the lips and their surrounding muscles which not only improve articulation but also serve to project the sound. As ever, Sir Hamilton was correct, I did learn many of the essential 'tricks of the trade'.

I attempted to show my admiration for Harty and his music when I had the opportunity of entering the recording studio in 1974 in order to record some songs for an anthology with which EMI marked my eightieth birthday. One record included a sequence of songs which commenced with a 1926 test record with Sir Hamilton at the piano, and which had not been previously published, and concluded with two of his finest songs accompanied by the ever remarkable and much missed Ivor Newton. It was extremely difficult to choose just two of the many beautiful songs Harty had written but I felt that the haunting *The stranger's grave* had to be included. I think the song ideally requires a warmer voice than mine, a voice with more drama to do it true justice. I was as dramatic as I could be but to my mind not quite enough.

On the other hand perhaps a dramatic voice could not have achieved the ethereal type of tone demanded by some of the higher lines.

I will never forget seeing 'Hay' at his London home in St John's Wood shortly after he had undergone a serious and what was to prove an unsuccessful operation. He asked me to sing to him and I obliged with his *Across the door*, a song I regularly included in my recitals devoted exclusively to his own compositions as well as in more general programmes. After the concluding *pianissimo* phrase 'his kiss upon my mouth' there was silence. Then, softly, he asked that I sing it again. We were both deeply moved and when I left there were tears in his eyes. He was taken back to Ireland and I never saw him again. His death in 1941 was a great personal blow as he had been such a loyal friend. He guided me, generally without my ever knowing. He was a remarkable man as well as a remarkable musician. It is sad that he is not now appreciated to the extent he deserves and that he still remains a somewhat shadowy figure when compared with so many of his exact contemporaries.

CHAPTER FOUR

On the Road

HAMILTON Harty provided me with my first professional break but it was Sir Henry Wood who enabled me to make my entrée into the capital. The London début was, as it remains to this day, one of the most critical landmarks in a musician's career and with Sir Henry at my side I considered myself most fortunate. I continued to have the pleasure of working with him for well over twenty years though our friendship did not become as close or as personal as my relationship with Harty.

Once again I have to thank the Fogg family for my introduction to Sir Henry. It materialised in a quite unexpected and roundabout manner. I think it was one Sunday in 1923 that I paid a courtesy visit to the Fogg household, where I discovered Eric busily preparing band parts for a concert to be given that afternoon in Harrogate by the Howard Carr Orchestra. I was riding on the crest of a wave, still flushed by the thrill of working with Harty and the Hallé on what was now a regular basis, though my appetite for singing with an orchestra remained insatiable. I consequently mentioned to Eric how I envied him and wished I too could accompany him to Harrogate and perform with the orchestra. No sooner mentioned than it was arranged! There would be no fee of course, simply a concert which would simultaneously act as an audition. I sang some Mozart, Micaëla's Act Three aria from *Carmen* and one or two other pieces, thoroughly enjoying myself into the bargain. When the concert was over Howard Carr kindly informed me that he intended to send a telegram the following day to Sir Henry Wood and William Boosey informing them that 'here was a singer they must on no account miss hearing'. I naturally thanked him though inwardly thought that I could readily forget all about that! But Howard Carr remained true to his word and a telegram was sent to London.

Within a short while I was duly summoned to London and gave an audition to Sir Henry and Mr Boosey in the Queen's Hall. Sir Henry was most kind and attentive, attempting to put me completely at ease. As I later discovered when I worked with him in numerous concerts, he was always naturally relaxed and genial and thoroughly professional. The audition proved successful and as a result I was awarded six Promenade Concert appearances during my first season in 1923. I continued to sing at the Proms in every subsequent season until the interruptions of the Second World War. Those early Prom appearances still provide me with many treasurable memories, not least an unforgettable Wagner night shared with Lauritz Melchior in his baritone days prior to his becoming the greatest Wagnerian *heldentenor* of his age.

The Proms were then held at the Queen's Hall. It was only after the hall was blitzed in 1941 that the concerts were transferred to the Royal Albert Hall. In Sir Henry's time the concerts adhered to a set pattern. Before the BBC took over the Proms in 1927 Monday night would be Wagner night and Friday night would be Beethoven, while the penultimate night would invariably include Beethoven's Choral Symphony. There would be no silly business on the last night either! Sir Henry would come on, take his bow and, after much applause, return with the evening's soloists. Finally he would reappear wearing his coat and carrying his hat: that was it, and all went home. There was very little audience participation at all in Sir Henry's time. It was, I think, Sir Malcolm Sargent who engendered all the 'fuzz-buzz'. I well remember one person saying after the first of the last night Prom performances in which Sir Malcolm allowed audience participation, 'He's going to regret this!', though I honestly think he never did.

After my introduction to the Proms Sir Henry took me back to some of the larger northern cities: a concert performance of *Lohengrin* at Leicester in which I sang Elsa, a programme of various operatic arias at Grimsby, a concert at the Morecambe Festival and such like. All proved to be exceptional musical experiences. On the train back to Manchester from Morecambe I encountered a little man who, on entering my compartment, looked at me most intently. Eventually he asked, 'Thar't Isobel Baillie aren't tha'?' 'Yes,' I replied with a smile. 'I'm on this 'ere Morecambe Festival Committee tha' knows,' he continued. My smile broadened a little though it fell somewhat when he continued, 'You know, when your name came up I said, Ee, is there nobuddy else?'

During my early work with Sir Henry he also gave me the opportunity to deputise for Carrie Tubb, then at the very peak of her career, in a concert at the People's Palace in the East End of London. Undoubtedly, though, one of the most impressive of all my concerts with Sir Henry took place in that other London palace, the Alexandra. This was a giant 'Handel Festival' devised by Sir Henry and given in June 1939 – he invited all the local choirs and a student orchestra to participate. My colleagues were Margaret Balfour, Frank Titterton and Harold Williams. We sang excerpts from *Israel in Egypt, Judas Maccabaeus* and *Messiah*, with the profits going towards the reconditioning of that building's monumental Willis organ. The sound of all the hundreds of participants was unbelievably thrilling and massive though I personally felt quite unable to reach the audience through the vast open space there; even the front seats seemed remote.

Nowadays one occasionally hears stories of Sir Henry being lax during rehearsals but I would emphasise that he was most punctilious in everything he did. He was always meticulous with his singers, ready to provide a piano rehearsal beforehand if he thought it needed or if requested. Provided one knew one's work there would be no trouble at all. If one didn't, look out! In one of his books he wrote of me that I was 'never anything but note perfect'. In essence that is a reflection of how he inspired a singer to do his or her homework.

Sir Henry also possessed an uncanny ability to suggest the right repertoire for a singer's temperament, ability and vocal range. During that first Prom season, at his suggestion, I sang *O come, do not delay* (*Deh vieni*) from *The Marriage of Figaro*, *I will extol thee* from Costa's *Eli*, *My heart ever faithful* from Bach's Cantata No. 68 as well as such songs, all to Sir Henry's splendidly atmospheric orchestrations, as Schubert's *Shepherd on the rock* and Grieg's *A dream* and *From Monte Pincio*. I owe him a deep debt of gratitude for introducing me to such splendid repertoire.

Sir Henry's legendary 'singer sympathy' was hardly surprising for someone who at the age of seventeen had set himself up in business as a teacher of singing and who had received singing lessons from just about every influential teacher of singing in this country at the end of the century, be it Gustav and Manuel Garcia, Randegger or Fiori. I once had a lesson from Sir Henry and his insight into the experience of vocal matters was, indeed, quite remarkable. His life's love and experience found expression in his penetrating and exhaustive treatise *The Gentle Art of Singing*. He was always unfailingly kind and regardful for his singers.

So, by the mid-1920s, I had completed my long apprenticeship in the North and had penetrated London. My name consequently became more familiar and the engagements began to tumble in. A full annual season would rapidly take shape. As can be imagined, for someone who so enjoyed her work and who always found it difficult to refuse an invitation, I would discover that my diary in reality was a little too full! London, of course, offered the Proms as well as appearances with the Royal Choral Society and Bach Choir. Then there were the annual festivals, be they at Leeds, Winchester or the cathedral cities of the Three Choirs Festival, though the bread and butter of the year's calendar was inevitably the concerts which were held throughout the length and breadth of the country. Naturally the most prestigious were the four principal regional orchestras, the Hallé, and those at Birmingham, Bournemouth and Liverpool. But there were also the enterprising summer orchestras to be found at the majority of seaside resorts: Blackpool, Hastings, Harrogate and Llandudno (where one year, when I sang there for an entire week, I discovered the season's conductor to be Malcolm Sargent!) plus Eastbourne, Scarborough, Torquay and Douglas, Isle of Man. All now, alas, are a lost part of musical history. Appearances at the resorts were generally kept to the proven formula of arias to orchestral accompaniment in the first half and a return to the platform during the second half to sing songs with piano accompaniment. I hope also that I did not forget my loyal Northern friends for I was only too pleased to sing for them – fewer in number perhaps than the audiencies of the crowded London Queen's Hall but just as warm and enthusiastic.

These engagements were not really properly arranged with specific areas being sensibly covered. Agents today are much more aware of 'blanket coverage', with meticulously planned tours of similar if not identical programmes. In my time engagements were simply accepted as and when they came in. The

consequence was a great contrast of repertoire and a tremendous
amount of travel, though not once did I ever think of questioning
the journeys such an approach entailed. It is only when I look
back over some of my surviving diaries that I discover the full
implication of such a haphazard approach. My schedule for December 1949, for example, ran:

1	Norwich
3	Edinburgh
4	Stockport
5	Broadstairs
6	Radcliffe
7	Swindon
8	Rawmarsh
9	Oxford
11	Manchester
12	Wolverhampton
13	Reading
14	Reading
15	Caernarvon
17	Liverpool
18	Liverpool
19	London (BBC)
20	London (Royal Albert Hall)
21	Bolton
22	Berwick-on-Tweed
26	Blackburn
30	Liverpool

while the following March it ran:

1	Birmingham
4	Macclesfield
5	Southend-on-Sea
8	Kirkcaldy
10	Bakewell
11	London (Hackney)
13	Diss
16	Cheltenham
17	London (Royal Albert Hall)
18	London (Royal Albert Hall)

19 Northampton
21 Devizes
22 Burton-on-Trent
23 Bristol
25 Bolton
26 London (Brixton)
27 London (Royal Albert Hall)
28 Woking
29 Liverpool
30 Bedford
31 Berkhamsted

Typical months in a typical year!

Such a work load was possible only because the amount of rehearsal required by most of these engagements was minimal. In those days, though more especially in the 1920s and 30s, rehearsals would take place only on the afternoon of the concert – even if the work in question was a long oratorio. Rehearsals the day before were rare and came into general currency only after the Second World War. Thus the morning, possibly even the night before, would be spent in travelling, hastily locating one's hotel and dashing to rehearsal. It was not exactly an unknown experience, particularly if the conductor was inclined to indulge himself, to come from the rehearsal with only enough time for a snatched cup of tea before it was time to dress for the performance. Recital engagements were a little less onerous largely because most of the preparation had been done at home. Naturally there would be a need for some kind of a run-through in order to acquaint oneself with the hall and its acoustics though it would only be necessary to rehearse the entire programme if one was working with an unfamiliar accompanist.

It was undoubtedly a hard and demanding existence, one which was possible only because I was fortunate enough to enjoy a strong constitution and good health. Even if I was so tired that I felt I could drop where I stood I was somehow always able to get to my boots for the actual performance. It was an attitude of mind amounting to self-deceit; I told myself that in just twenty minutes all would be over and then it *would* be possible to collapse somewhere out of sight.

Inevitably there were hazards. Verbal, even written instructions could become garbled though only once did I arrive at a venue to discover I was expected to sing a work other than that which I had prepared. This nightmarish experience happened shortly after the war in, I think, Maidstone. I arrived prepared to sing one of Vaughan Williams's major choral works only to discover that the programme stated that Isobel Baillie was to sing *and narrate* Vaughan Williams's *Song of thanksgiving*, a work I neither knew nor had even heard! All I could do in the four or five hours left before the performance was to knuckle down, learn the soprano role and make myself familiar with the not inconsiderable amount of text which I was expected to narrate.

Certain aspects of appearing in public are, understandably, generally taken for granted, not least the manner in which a singer dresses; yet this too has to be learnt, sometimes the hard way. I discovered what to wear and what not to wear by watching other artists during my early years, though I only became truly aware of the importance of being correctly dressed after an appearance at a Saturday afternoon Boosey Ballad Concert in the mid-1920s. Mr Boosey came up to me, clutching a manuscript, and said 'I'd like you to sing this new ballad for me', adding, almost as an afterthought, 'Oh, and perhaps you could find a new dress for the occasion.' The remark was like a gun shot. Instantly the thought came into my head that I had not been looking right on stage. I used to wear dresses which I had considered most appropriate but obviously they were not quite what was expected. From that time on I took infinite trouble with my appearance on the concert platform.

I became a regular customer of a splendid fashion shop in St Anne's Square, Manchester, where the buyer took an interest in me and whose advice was to prove invaluable particularly after one of my earliest personal attempts at *haute couture* had misfired. I had purchased a magnificent satin dress in a superb mauve which I thought would suit my colouring and which boasted a most decorous silver flower on the corsage. It was only when I appeared on the platform that I discovered that the stage lights transformed the mauve into a quite disgusting shade of grey!

My very first evening dress was actually given to me by a friend of my mother's, a reward for winning a vocal competition (incidentally, the only competition I ever entered) at the Albert Hall, Manchester, during my early teens. It was made of Swiss embroidery and was adorned with a pale blue sash. I was the bee's knees in my first 'posh dress'. I also remember the pale blue chiffon evening dress I wore for my Hallé début and my sense of disappointment at being positioned so far away from the audience: I perhaps need not have taken quite so much care over my appearance! But this was uncharacteristic thinking for I always aimed to look my best irrespective of whether the engagement was major or not. I still feel that one should dress up for an occasion. When the engagement book began to bulge it became necessary, so I thought, to make a note of what dress had been worn and where though I was frequently teased by my female collegues that this was quite unnecessary because I bought far too many dresses.

Leisure time, a most precious commodity, was generally spent at the cinema and theatre; in a word, escapism! I mentioned earlier how the cinema lured me almost from infancy. My addiction could not be assuaged, rather it grew with age and sometimes by some miracle or other I would be able to squeeze in two or three visits to the cinema in a single week. My love for the theatre can be traced back to childhood trips to the music hall at Hulme Hippodrome in Manchester where I would sit enthralled by the vigour and excitement which leapt across the footlights and pinned me to my seat. Later, when I had more time to indulge myself, I would manage at least a couple of theatre visits in a week especially when the National Theatre first opened on the South Bank. I don't think I missed a single production during those halcyon early years.

Naturally a full engagement diary meant that the days of scrimping and saving were over, though never at any stage in my career did I ever earn enough to feel affluent. This was partly because the fees earned then were always comparatively modest – only in the most exceptional circumstances did my fee ever top forty guineas. From my fee agent's commission and all expenses had to be deducted. What was left could then be spent upon the family. There was also one further inescapable fact: my standards exceeded my income! As I have just mentioned I liked the best clothes and I enjoyed the best food. I would consequently sacrifice to attain such things and I did not even contemplate saving until I neared the end of my singing career. If one insists on high standards money has to be spent! Where these standards came from I do not know as my childhood can only be described as frugal. I am left with the thought that it is something inborn and that sampling is dangerously addictive.

With cash available it became possible to rent a cottage in order to escape the hurly-burly and recharge my batteries. Harry and I considered ourselves extremely fortunate when we discovered a cottage near Silecroft idyllically situated in the Breast of Black-combe above Barrow. It came fully equipped with pond and attendant ducks together with an orchard. I went to the sales in Manchester and bought the most beautiful bedroom set for two pounds. It had originally been in a theatre and, most unusually, was white with inlaid Wedgewood plaques on the wardrobe doors. The cottage provided me with my first opportunity of withdrawing from the everyday demands of life. I was able to rest and read and Harry was able to fish in the estuary of the River Solway to his heart's content. More often than not he returned triumphant with a handsome salmon. We both relished the countryside. It had been in my blood since those carefree childhood holidays spent at Bowhill when I could sling a ham-mock between two trees and spend hours in a suspended dream world. It was also at Bowhill that I learnt to 'gump' a trout: tickling it with the fingers until it drifts into a state of hypnotic tranquillity when it can be lifted straight out of the water.

But there comes a time when even escaping to the countryside is not enough, when a total and complete break is required. Such was my mood during the winter of 1932, a feeling of being totally and utterly drained. It was Harry who came up with the highly attractive proposition of visiting my brother Alex in Honolulu. I entertained the idea very seriously for it had been far too long since I had seen Alex and there was much news to exchange. And besides, the very name Honolulu conjured up a warm, romantic haven, certainly a place I wished to discover for myself. Once the thought had been planted in my mind there was no stopping me and my brain began to teem with ideas, one of the foremost being to sing at the Hollywood Bowl, then one of the newer American wonders. Surely as I would be travelling so near it was worth a try! I mentioned this somewhat hair-brained scheme to Sir Hamilton and Sir Henry, both of whom had conducted at the Bowl, and they considered it an idea well worth pursuing. Harty in particular gave me much encouragement as he was due to conduct there in the not-too-distant future.

It was not long before I set out from England on what was only the second holiday trip of my life. I was duly armed with letters of recommendation from both Harty and Wood, buoyant at the prospect of seeing Alex again and at the thought of having an extended rest period, and I was also inwardly excited by the remote possibility of my singing at the Bowl. When I reached Hollywood the presentation of my letters instantly transformed me into a VIP. There were breakfasts with committee members, dinners with high-powered organisers and the like; everyone was exceptionally kind, though as the days passed nothing was ever mentioned concerning an audition for an appearance at the Bowl. I was somewhat disarmed but felt that I was in no position to act the 'pushy' soprano and thus run the risk of antagonising all around me. My only option was to play a waiting game. Meanwhile there was, of course, plenty to see and do. I was taken to the MGM studios and given an extended grand tour. The talkies had only recently burst onto an astonished world and as I walked through the vast MGM empire I passed row upon row of little singing studios each containing an aspiring young actress painfully discovering that singing was both a mysterious and unattainable art. I was also given a chaperone in the form of Ivy St Hellier. She was of great assistance especially when I was suddenly called upon to pose for some photographs. To my consternation they dragged on a camel from a nearby set and it fell to my lot to pose with my unattractive and highly disgruntled partner. Ivy was invaluable; she told me how I should stand, how to hold my hands, position my head and so on. All the while the poor beast moaned and spat. I knew how it felt, inwardly I was doing the same. I never did see the resultant 'shots'. Perhaps they still lurk in some forgotten Hollywood basement.

I also saw many of the legendary screen idols in action and even met some of them in off-screen moments: Cary Grant, for example, badly in need of a shave and concentrating on the demolition of a hamburger and beer. I was finally taken 'upstairs' to see 'the great man' who I think was the chief director, though pleasantries were basically all that were exchanged between us. I think it became obvious to all around that I was not exactly bursting to break into Hollywood!

I stayed at the Hollywood Hotel which even then was considered to be an old-fashioned establishment of 'outstanding charm'. It was one of the smaller buildings in that most extraordinary town with a superb balcony running all round it. Needless to say, I saw many movies in Hollywood including one of the very first big musicals, currently showing at Grauman's Chinese

Theatre situated just next door to my hotel, and, like every other tourist, I inspected the pavement outside the theatre where the celebrated left their footprints for posterity. Superficially all was breathless excitement yet inwardly I grew more and more disappointed as there were still no signs of any approach from the Hollywood Bowl. By the penultimate day of my Hollywood sojourn I had more or less given up all hope but then, out of the blue, a representative came to see me with a contract in his hand. Much to my astonishment I was not even asked to give an audition, merely to sign a contract with the romantically named 'Symphonies under the Stars Foundation', which specified the not unattractive sum of $250 for a single appearance. My introductory letters from Harty and Wood were obviously enough. I was to be taken on trust.

After my holiday in Honolulu I returned to Hollywood where on 27 July 1933 I made my American début in a concert with Sir Hamilton Harty. I thus had the honour of being the first British singer ever to perform at the Hollywood Bowl. It was a magnificent setting, an absolutely natural amphitheatre with a seating capacity of twenty-five thousand – if there were some empty seats that night it was still the largest 'live' audience I ever faced in my entire career. Hills rose up on all sides of the bowl, with an open-fronted concert platform, centrally positioned. There were no microphones or loudspeakers, the amplification being entirely natural, yet the sound was quite superb. Facing such a vast open space I imagined that the sound would fade before me but miraculously my voice carried just as it did in the concert hall. It had all proved most invigorating and I returned to England totally refreshed and ready for the next season.

CHAPTER FIVE

More Conductors

THE overall pattern of my life as a singer can now, I hope, be envisaged with little difficulty. On paper the regularity and routine of my work might appear to some rather monotonous, perhaps even mundane, though in practice it transpired to be nothing less than enjoyable and, more often than not, stimulating and invigorating. But to recall in chronological detail the floodtide of work during the 1930s, 40s and 50s would be far too repetitive. I have consequently opted to devote the following three chapters to some specific 'thrills and spills' of those years according to their relevance to the three types of musicians with whom I have worked. Naturally there are my peers, the singers; we strange hybrid creatures! Each member of the species is as different as chalk from cheese as indeed they must be, for vocal individuality so essential for true success is born only of personal individuality. Then there is the composer, who has provided me with so many musical highlights of my life and whose presence has crowned many an auspicious occasion. But first I must salute the conductor, the indefatigable major-domo of music. He is, after all, the unfortunate creature who has to accept the overall responsibility for a musical performance.

My work with Hamilton Harty and Henry Wood has already been described, for my career was launched under their extraordinarily sympathetic batons. With them the foundations were laid. But it will come as no surprise to those who know me when I state that the crucial building upon those foundations was largely done under the supervision of one man, Malcolm Sargent.

I must have sung more with Sir Malcolm than with any other

conductor. This was the man who, as an unknown organist in his mid-twenties from Lincolnshire, took London by storm from the moment he conducted his own *Allegro impetuoso*, entitled *An impression of a windy day*, at a 1921 Henry Wood Promenade concert. During the ensuing decade success appeared to crown success and it must have been towards the end of this initial flush of glory that we first worked together. As a conductor his approach was fundamentally different from that of either Wood or Harty, both of whom built up, in their vastly differing ways, personal relationships with their orchestras. Sir Henry, for example, waged a long and arduous battle to put an end to the 'deputy system' – the method by which a conductor would rehearse a group of players in the morning only to be faced by a vast array of strange faces ('deputies') at the actual concert. Sargent was quite different. I do not think he particularly cared *who* was in front of him provided they played the notes in the required manner. This was undoubtedly because he did not develop any personal feelings towards his orchestra. This is not, however, to suggest that he was remote or unemotional, rather that he was ultra-professional, someone who could control an assembly of musicians with cool authority. 'Emotion' would come only from the music in front of him and then in a restrained manner. His accompaniments, particularly in concertos, were models of their kind, totally at one with the soloist and full of feeling though never of the self-indulgent kind.

Sir Malcolm, contrary to popular belief, certainly had feelings. Nowhere was this more graphically evident than during the war-torn 1940s when his daughter, Pamela, lay dying. She had contracted infantile paralysis as a teenager in 1938 and after a remarkable recovery, had suffered what appeared to be an irreversible and agonisingly slow decline. Her death, in 1944 when she was twenty, proved to be the grief of Sargent's life; some maintain he was never quite the same again. It was during this sad period that we gave a performance of Berlioz's *The Childhood of Christ* in Liverpool. I had a morning piano rehearsal with him in the basement of the Adelphi Hotel and after commencing the Virgin's solo, *See darling child*, a most tender and gentle moment, I happened to look at him. His accompaniment had not faltered but tears were streaming down his face. He used, apparently, to sit for long spells at his daughter's bedside, the fruits of these vigils being his atmospheric and poignant orchestration of

49

Brahms's *Four Serious Songs*, which were so superbly sung both by Kathleen Ferrier and Nancy Evans.

Sargent's reticence, so frequently misinterpreted as off-handedness, was even reflected in his acts of kindness which were always so quietly executed. I recall a particularly demanding recording session in 1947 at the Kingsway Hall which included the recording of *Where art thou, father dear?* from Dvořák's *The Spectre's Bride* and *The sun goeth down* from *The Kingdom*, demanding enough in their own right but doubly so when the necessary alternative 'takes' had to be made. By the end of the allocated three hours I was near to the point of collapse. Sargent's remedy, done with the absolute minimum of fuss, was to bundle me into a taxi and to take me to the Savoy Grill where he insisted that I drank champagne. It was the most demonstrable act he ever showed me. Astonishing as it may seem, although we worked together on literally countless occasions throughout the British Isles, he always called me 'Miss Baillie' while I invariably addressed him as 'Sir Malcolm'. His cultivated veneer, distancing him from those with whom he worked, be they orchestral musicians or soloists, contributed, I would say, towards making him such a fine conductor, a figure not fully appreciated in the years since his death.

I will also never forget a performance of *Elijah* which we gave in the darkest days of the Depression during the 1930s in South Wales. The 'artists' room' was exceptionally primitive and included an earthen floor, but the massive local choir was truly wonderful and the resultant performance indelibly memorable. When the opening chorus, *Help! Lord! wilt thou quite destroy us?* commenced it was like something one had never heard before: these poor people were literally addressing the heavens for assistance. Even Sargent was impressed; after the performance he exclaimed in true astonishment, 'Have you ever heard a chorus sing like that before?'

It will come as no surprise when I mention that the most colourful and entertaining conductor I have ever sung with was Sir Thomas Beecham. He always provided value for money wherever and whenever I sang with him, and it was both a great joy and satisfaction to sing with him whether at the festivals of Edinburgh, Norwich and Leeds or at concerts up and down of the country. Every occasion left an exciting memory, many of which are recalled elsewhere in these pages.

Beecham and Baillie generally met in oratorio, for he was a great and natural champion of the great English choral tradition. On the only occasion I sang Haydn's *Creation* with him my enthusiasm for the genre in general and *The Creation* in particular was perhaps revealed a little too earnestly, for after we had rehearsed *On mighty pens* he turned to me, beamed and said, 'You like singing that, don't you?' I, of course, agreed. (But even making comments *during* a performance was nothing out of the ordinary at a Beecham concert; there was the time when he leant towards me at a Queen's Hall performance of Brahms's *German Requiem* during the chorus *All flesh is as grass* and said in a bored voice, 'This is a *dull* piece!') One thing has always puzzled me concerning that performance of *The Creation*, namely why he did not allow me to sing the role of Eve, preferring instead to import another soprano, in this instance Olive Groves. He obviously did not see me as Eve, but to this day I am not quite sure whether this should be regarded as a compliment or not!

Beecham's wit was legendary, as deft as the way he played those miniatures of the French repertoire in which he so delighted. A classic example, and one which I have not seen in print, concerned a young musician, John Hollingsworth, then making his initial, exploratory steps as a conductor. Someone told Sir Thomas during a visit to their town that Hollingsworth was due to conduct the next concert of their winter season. Did Sir Thomas know of this man? How did Sir Thomas think he would fare? Beecham, without pause, looked the enquirer straight in the eye and growled somewhat testily 'Conductors are born not Hollingsworth!' I was never subsequently able to pass the London store of Bourne and Hollingsworth without thinking of Sir Thomas!

The last time I worked with Beecham was at the Edinburgh Festival in a performance of Haydn's *The Seasons*. During the interval he lolled back in his chair and proclaimed as only 'T.B.' *could* proclaim, 'Here I am in Scotland yet I can't find a decent glass of whisky.' The inevitable happened and the committee began to buzz around in mild confusion. We returned to the platform and completed the performance which, incidentally, showed no signs of being any the worse for Sir Thomas's deficiency. After we had all taken our bows I noticed two committee members making an effortful way to the centre of the stage manhandling a large box, bedecked with an obvious red ribbon, which we later discovered contained an assortment of Scotland's finest whisky. Sir Thomas's astonishment quickly gave way to a satisfied grin when he realised the contents of this surprise package. He simply placed the box on his head and stalked off the platform. It was the last time I ever saw him.

I worked far less with Adrian Boult, though this was not from choice but simply the way things happened. One vivid memory of Sir Adrian I do possess, however, was at yet another performance of *Elijah* at an Eisteddfod. We were singing in an enormous marquee and as the performance was about to start we noticed storm clouds gathering. When Elijah, naturally sung by Harold Williams, called, *Open the heavens and send us relief: Help thy servant now O God!* the atmosphere was stiflingly close and heavy; then, as I sang the Youth's *The heavens are black with cloud and wind: the storm rusheth louder and louder*, so did the heavens literally open, the lashing rain almost drowning out Elijah's gratitude *Thanks be to God for all his mercies!* Earlier in my career I had the impression that Sir Adrian tended to favour orchestral precision rather than interpretative inspiration, quite the reverse of his later performances which were truly inspired, particularly his Elgar which I think I prefer to all others. Sir Adrian, it hardly needs stating, was always very gentlemanly and never interfered with one's singing or approach.

I worked with Stanford Robinson, 'Robbie' as he is known to all his friends, far more frequently. His true standing as a conductor was always inclined to be underestimated even during his heyday in the 1930s. Later he became somewhat overshadowed by the television success of his brother Eric, though there can be no doubting Stanford's superior talent. He did a colossal amount of work for the BBC in various capacities, including being the first conductor of the BBC Choral Society in 1928 when it was known as the National Chorus. I well remember coming down to London week after week to participate in a series devoted to Bach's cantatas, sometimes simply to sing a recitative. It is a matter of great regret that so little of his conducting survives. I think the first time I ever worked with him was in February 1930 when among other things we recorded *Elijah* for Columbia with Harold Williams, Clara Serena and Parry Jones. In the following September, recording some popular titles including *The doll's song* from *The Tales of Hoffmann*, nothing, for some reason, would go right. I began to despair of ever being able to sing the piece in what was to me a satisfactory manner. Robbie came to the rescue. For the one and only time in all the many occasions we subsequently worked together he melted, put his arm around my shoulder and said encouragingly, 'Now come along, you can do it!' If it was a rare display of affection it was most aptly timed and did the trick.

This gesture was recalled by him well over ten years later in a letter which I received just before a broadcast of Gounod's *Faust* which he was directing. I quote it in full for it says much about his care and concern, not only for the singers with whom he worked but also for the music he conducted.

Isobel darling,

    Just a note to wish you a great personal success tonight. I can't help knowing that the rehearsals have given you some worrying moments. [We had experienced some problems with the balance during the final rehearsal.] I am sorry, for when I heard from Gladys Ripley of your great success as Marguerite in New Zealand I made a mental vow to invite you to sing it for me at its next broadcast. We had such a happy rehearsal together on Sunday morning and I was very pleased when the day was over for I felt we were of one mind. Since then I have had so many other things and people to deal with that our contact has not been so intimate but remember at the show tonight that my chief care is to help you to give one of the best performances, if not the *best*, of your career. Sing to *me* and with *me*. May I add a few reminders as from an old broadcasting hand to an old friend. Remember that although the microphone has no eye, your facial expression affects the colour of your voice so *act all* the time: laugh, cry, smile, scream, shudder just as if you were in the theatre and your voice will reflect it all. *Remember that the softer you sing the more distinctly you must speak.* Throw your words as far as me and the mike will get them too.

    Finally, remember in your top notes not to emulate the flute, but the stringy notes of the violin as you did *beautifully* for me on Sunday. It is so much more expressive.

    You'll think me an awful bore for saying all this. You want to be a success. I want you to be a success. I want you to want to do another opera too.

    Remember the record of The doll's song and imagine I've got my arm around you.

Good luck and God bless.

Much love
Robbie.

P.S.   Sorry I have to cut the second verse of Thule but we should overrun if we sang it.

It is a great paradox that I was destined to sing so rarely with John Barbirolli considering I lived in Manchester for most of my life and that Sir John conducted the Hallé from 1943 until his death in 1970. The only work I ever sang with him was Finzi's *Dies natalis* which we sang twice in Manchester and repeated in Sheffield and Bradford. Barbirolli was, of course, famous for his way with strings and I will always treasure his beautiful and responsive accompaniment to that work: the hushed anticipation of *The corn was orient and immortal wheat which never should be reap'd nor was even sown*, the sublime tranquillity of *Everything was at rest, free and immortal* and the dancing playfulness of *Sweet infancy*.

Before I leave the subject of British conductors I must mention the very first encounter I ever had with any prestigious conductor. This was with Landon Ronald and must have taken place in my late teens. Although now very much a peripheral figure Sir Landon was enormously influential in his day: conductor and accompanist to Melba, conductor of grand opera at Drury Lane and of the orchestras in Vienna, Amsterdam and Leipzig, composer and, to boot, Principal of the Guildhall School of Music. And here I stood before this man at Forsyths, Manchester's largest musical shop, about to sing an audition. After I had performed my piece he made approving and appreciative noises and laid emphatic stress on the idea that he thought I would do particularly well in musical comedy. I was totally affronted at such an idea and found it even difficult to thank him for his time!

This was not, however, the only time I was advised to pursue a similar path. Much later I was summoned to London by Lady Utica Beecham and Sir Thomas's son Adrian and after an audition offered the part of Portia in Adrian's opera based upon Shakespeare's *Merchant of Venice* scheduled for production at the Duke of York's Theatre. By this time I was far from being affronted, realising that variety is indeed the spice of one's career, but acceptance would have meant giving up so much work, which I could ill afford to do, in order to undertake a month's rehearsal period. Somewhat reluctantly I was obliged to decline.

It was also my immense privilege to work with some of the most illustrious international conductors. During my career music-making was, of course, much less internationally based than it is now. The great advancements in travel have made it possible to perform in New York one day and London the next, though from a musical stand-point one is forced to question

54

whether this is actually an advantage. In the 1920s and 30s visiting
international soloists and conductors were more the exception
than the rule and frequently the announcement of a visit from a
foreign celebrity would prompt advance bookings of a quite exceptional volume. I think the most exciting conductor I have *ever*
worked with was Victor de Sabata, a far too infrequent visitor to
these shores. He was the man who succeeded Toscanini as Artistic
Director of La Scala, Milan, in 1929 though he did not visit
Britain until after the Second World War when he made some
astonishing appearances with the London Philharmonic Orchestra. He somehow brought new life to the most familiar work and
his technical command was incomparable; he would rehearse the
most complex piece without a score. This was so when I sang in
a never-to-be-forgotten performance of Beethoven's Choral Symphony. I am not sure whether it was because he was so meticulous
about every minute detail but he would go over everything time
and time again, all with infinite patience, yet all the time conducting at white-hot intensity. For all the repetition involved,
working for him was never boring. If it proved fearsomely demanding, it was also highly invigorating. I have participated in
countless performances of the Choral Symphony, a work for
which I have to admit, sacrilegious though it might appear, I do
not have a particular fondness, yet that performance with de
Sabata was undoubtedly the most exciting and thrilling I have
ever taken part in.

Still with the Choral Symphony, I am reminded of a performance in which I participated with Kathleen Ferrier, Heddle Nash
and William Parsons, conducted by Bruno Walter. I cannot honestly say that it was an enjoyable experience as I felt Walter had
little sympathy with my voice. He was, of course, much more
interested in Kathleen who was at that time very close to him. I
recently discovered, with some consternation, that the performance, given in the Royal Albert Hall in November 1947, was
somehow recorded complete and is now in general circulation.

Another conductor capable of giving a both penetrating and
exciting performance was Eduard van Beinum. This quite magnificent musician was another conductor brought to this country
by the London Philharmonic, and he became its conductor for a
few valued years from 1949. I had the inestimable pleasure of
singing Bach's St Matthew Passion under his baton. He seemed

to be an exceptional Bach interpreter, unfolding the performance with unerring instinct and insight.

Sometimes a visitor would stay for a period of several weeks in order to perform a whole series of concerts. Toscanini, for example, once he had left the New York Philharmonic, was able to make an annual extended visit to Britain during the late 1930s. These visitations were generally preceded by a full week of intensive rehearsals. Concertos were rarely included, although the maestro did require vocalists for several choral works. In 1937 London buzzed with excitement when Toscanini's visit was announced. However when I received a telephone call at my club in Cavendish Square asking if I would go to the Queen's Hall with my score of Brahms's *German Requiem* and sing for Toscanini I can honestly say that it came quite out of the blue. Toscanini had, up to that time, never worked with British singers before and we consequently surmised that he would bring his soloists with him. Naturally I went. I discovered Barclay Mason seated at the piano on stage and the great man, together with Madam Toscanini, positioned in the front row of the stalls. He asked me to sing the brief but demanding solo *Ihr habt nun Traurigkeit*, that sublime movement added after the work's first performance. After I had finished he said very little but took both my hands in his and said 'Bene, bene!' I, in turn, thanked him for listening and sped on my way somewhat relieved that the ordeal had not proved quite as worriesome as I had imagined, though more or less putting the idea of singing for Toscanini firmly out of my mind: after all there would surely be an endless stream of sopranos waiting to give an audition. Much to my surprise, however, I quickly discovered that I was to be Toscanini's soprano for that performance of the Brahms *Requiem* on 30 October 1937 with Alexander Sved as baritone soloist. Toscanini also asked me to sing in Beethoven's Choral Symphony in the same series of concerts. This took place on 3 November 1937, an all-Beethoven evening which commenced with the First Symphony; my confrères were Mary Jarred, Parry Jones and Harold Williams.

Toscanini was by repute an impossible martinet. However, I experienced no symptoms of this – not once did he ask me to do anything in any way different from what I had always done. As a vocal quartet in the Beethoven we were, however, reminded not to forget the *poco* qualification to the *adagio* marking at the point 'Alle Menschen werden Brüder' which marks the beginning

56

of the final solo quartet. 'Poco, poco, poco adagio', he insisted.
I have to confess that I had never much thought about that *poco*
marking but what a difference it made – it was so much easier to
sing!

Earlier in the movement Harold Williams had unwittingly
drawn Toscanini into revealing his thoughts about one of his
close contemporaries and rivals! Harold was revelling in the florid
writing of the bass recitative, *O Freunde, nicht diese Töne!* When
he approached the dramatic coloratura of the final word 'freuden-
vollere!' he took a leonine stance, lifted his chest and sang the
entire phrase in one magnificent breath. Toscanini stopped, put
down his baton and bowed his head. After a moment he pulled
himself erect, his eyes transfixing Harold to the spot with an
ominous glance. 'You boast!', he curtly proclaimed. Harold, with
some justification, was nonplussed. 'Well, Maestro,' he began,
desperately searching for excuses, 'when I last sang it like that a
few weeks ago,' he continued, getting ever nearer to the edge of
the precipice, 'Koussevitzky liked it and . . . '. The excuse petered
out into forlorn silence. The atmosphere was electric. Slowly
Toscanini's face assumed a puzzled, vacant expression. 'Koussevitzky?' he queried in childlike innocence. 'Koussevitzky?' he repeated looking for assistance from the assembled orchestra. Then
the light dawned and the face began to register some degree of
recall. 'Ah yes [pause], Koussevitzky [even longer pause] he
played the contrabass!' Quite true, of course, for the only way
Koussevitzky had been able to gain entrance into the Moscow
Conservatoire was by entering the double bass class where there
happened to be a vacancy.

Toscanini possessed an incredible magnetism and seemed to
secure the very best from all his musicians. Naturally one always
felt that one had to be constantly on one's toes and I would have
hated to have made a mistake. Although he was extremely strict
with his orchestral players I never saw him being unkind. His aim
was always the meticulous, flawless interpretation of the score as
he saw it.

I was later told by a friend that after the Brahms performance
someone at the BBC asked Toscanini how he liked the English
soprano. Apparently he replied, 'Right in the middle of the note
and none of this' – waving his hands in and out as if playing a
concertina. In those days an excessive vibrato, quite rightly I
think, was severely frowned upon (nevertheless it was much in

evidence in certain quarters). When Toscanini returned to this country in May 1939 to participate in the London Music Festival at which the BBC Symphony Orchestra played all the Beethoven symphonies, seven of them with Toscanini, it was a renewed joy to sing the Choral Symphony under his baton.

My agents, Ibbs and Tillett, were responsible for the interpretation of all the small print in the contract for the Toscanini concerts. They showed me that it specified I should keep the week prior to the performances free in order that I might attend any rehearsals Toscanini would call. When I pointed out that I already had three engagements that week I was told in no uncertain manner that if I wanted to participate in the Toscanini concerts I would have to forego these bookings. I tried to resist, stating that I could attend any day rehearsals required – after all, not even Toscanini could rehearse during the evening and conduct the concerts too! – and still honour my long-standing commitments. I even went to the BBC to beard the Booking Manager in his den. I stated my case: 'Do you realise', I explained, 'that I am going to lose three engagements during this week, a week in which I might possibly not even be called to attend rehearsals!' His reply was predictable, 'Don't *you* realise that countless sopranos would give half their annual salary to be doing this concert. You ought to consider yourself lucky that you are doing this at all.' It was an attitude which riled me and, gritting my teeth, I reminded him that I had actually attended an audition. This quietened him a little but I lost the battle and it was with some embarrassment that I was forced to cancel earlier arrangements. It was an approach which was typical of this time and a great contrast from today when what the artist says goes. To crown it all I did not even receive a rehearsal fee from the BBC, simply my usual fee of £30. Small wonder that I am neither rich nor basking in luxury!

I often wonder if the public realise what a crucial role the agent plays in shaping an artist's career and subsequent fortunes. In retrospect I am sure my agents could have secured far more than my top fee of forty guineas. When I did pluck up enough courage to confront them the reply was invariably, 'Well, that's the fee they pay.' Perhaps things would have been different if I had not had to manage my own affairs but could have fallen back on the support of someone who could have taken a stand, someone who would have declared with a masculine threat, 'She's not going to sing for that!'

Sometimes it was almost necessary to bully one's agent into approaching concert organisers as, for example, when I wished to participate in the Sunday ballad concerts at the Coliseum which were very much part of London's musical life in the 1920s. I approached Mr Tillett and asked if he could secure an engagement for me there; having attended some of these concerts I was confident that I could reach the required standard! 'Ah, Miss Baillie', came his reply, 'At present you're an attraction but not a draw.' If the name did not persuade people to part with their money and fill the house then that was it. One was engaged simply to secure an audience. I eventually managed to prove myself in the interim and crossed that mysterious, invisible dividing line to share my first bill with the legendary Ben Davies, famed for his white gloves which were as immaculate as his ballad singing and even worn in the recording studio!

It also transpired that a London based agency was not always *au fait* with what a North country girl was up to! Shortly after I started to sing regularly in London I had quite a talk with John Tillett who said in the course of conversation, 'I suppose we secure most of your engagements, Miss Baillie.' 'Oh yes', I replied, 'About ten per cent!' He was truly shocked. I secured the remaining ninety per cent by word of mouth predominantly from my North Country connections. John Tillett also, it appeared, used to take a pride in telling interested parties that it really was no use asking for Isobel Baillie as she had an engagement nearly every night of the year! I also learnt later that requests to sing in Holland had to be refused due to my heavy UK commitments.

But to return to Toscanini. I must share with the reader a personal glimpse of this man which proves that on no matter how high a pedestal we place some artists they still remain human, suffering the same foibles and, in this instance, the same anxieties as we ordinary mortals. The 1937 performance of the Choral Symphony was attended by the Duke and Duchess of Kent who, for some reason, were delayed. We four singers were foregathered in a little alcove just off-stage. Mary took advantage of the only armchair while I perched myself on the arm. Parry and Harold were standing; Harold, as ever, straight as a die. Toscanini was pacing restlessly up and down in front of us looking more and more nervous and tense. Suddenly it all became too much for him. He turned to face us, his baton disconsolately held in one hand and a mournful expression on his face, and moaned, 'What a life!' with a hapless shrug of the shoulders. Musical gods *are* human.

CHAPTER SIX

Singing Colleagues

IT WAS not particularly easy to get to know one's singing colleagues. Circumstances were generally set against such luxuries
for we normally came across each other only during rehearsals
and concerts; for the rest of the time we were scurrying around
the country – usually in opposite directions. Occasionally if we
coincidentally found ourselves staying at the same hotel we would
have supper together but this was very much the exception to the
rule. Generally friendships could only grow over a long time
when, year after year, we would meet at such annual gatherings
as the Three Choirs or the Sheffield Festivals.

The singers I remember from my early years could not even be
described as acquaintances. They were shadowy figures at the
peak of their careers whom I briefly encountered on stage during
my first faltering footsteps. Yet it is quite extraordinary how
some of their voices remain forever locked in the memory. I can,
for instance, still hear in my mind some of the singers I heard
during those highly impressionable days at the start of my career
in the North. Annie Hargreaves was one such artist. She possessed
a contralto voice of quite exceptional beauty: feminine, warm and
creamily voluptuous. We first met at a local concert in Manchester
and I was so impressed by her sound that I persuaded Sir Hamilton
to hear her. He, likewise, was equally captivated and gave her a
Hallé *Messiah* but we were, alas, both sadly disappointed from
a musical point of view; when she sang an aria such as *He was
despised* it seemed quite interminable. She realised, I think, that
the 'big time' was not really for her and remained quite content
with her many and always successful local engagements.

Among the men I remember from this era was Hamilton Harris, arguably at this time the most prominent bass-baritone in the North. He was a soloist at my second Hallé concert which took place on 9 April 1922 at the Free Trade Hall with Harty conducting. Harris had a sturdy voice and an ample range though it had no special 'character', so essential for a really big career. What strikes me so forcibly when I now look at that programme was Hamilton Harris's extraordinary wide repertoire: in the first half he contributed, by request, *The trumpet shall sound* and a collection of songs in part two comprising Ernest Austin's *Life*, Wolf's *Anacreon's grave* and Korbay's *Had a horse!* (the last was a popular contemporary novelty). Hamilton Harris also frequently sang for Beecham when the conductor ventured North. His daughter, Nancy, is now a familiar and popular accompanist, and adjudicates at Northern competitions.

I also remember being in the same programme at the Free Trade Hall with Tom Burke and his wife, Marie, when they returned to this country for the first time after an extensive period of study in Italy. They were nervous and rather on edge, only too aware of the importance of the occasion, but they need have had no qualms for Tom in particular carved for himself a regarded career in opera and musicals.

The tenor with whom I sang most frequently in my earliest days was Frank Mullings. I think he was basically a born singer who had not fully learnt his trade; I remain convinced that he did not know a great deal about singing and that most of his work was instinctive. He was, however, an extremely clever artist and an amazing actor, dramatically involved to the very core and truly living the part. His Otello, the role by which he is now largely remembered, was deeply impressive, his great and impressive stature proving so apt for the part. It is regrettable that his recordings of the role give only a partial glimpse of this great assumption, though we can gain some idea of the size of his voice as well as his ability to sing an exquisite *pianissimo*. He was also a very fine Canio in *I Pagliacci* and Radamès in *Aida* and he conquered many Wagnerian roles too. He was, for example, the first English Parsifal and a notable Tristan. Frank was a particularly easy man to work with which probably explains why Beecham adored him so. In his autobiography, *A Mingled Chime*, Beecham writes so accurately and perceptively about Mullings

62

that it deserves to be reiterated here. Of Mullings's vocal method Beecham categorically states that:

> I do not think he ever had one at all, and when he tackled, or rather stormed certain high passages in *Otello*, *Aida* or *Tristan*, I used to hold my breath in apprehension of some dire physical disaster, averted only by the possession of an iron frame that permitted him to play tricks which would have sent any other tenor into hospital for weeks. But in the centre his voice had ease and uncommon beauty, and his singing of quiet passages had a poetry, spirituality, and intelligence which I have never heard in any other native artist and very few elsewhere.

After the First World War we used to visit hospitals and camps together where we would sing to the wounded. He particularly enjoyed our duets and was most anxious for me to sing Elsa to his Lohengrin, something unfortunately we were never able to realise.

Another singer who, like Annie Hargreaves, lacked an ambitious drive but who possessed a splendid soprano voice was Anne Chadwick, known to all her friends and colleagues as 'Nan'. She has been a close friend of mine since we met in Italy where we were both studying with Somma. Once again Hamilton Harty was the instigation behind such a move. I found myself taking her under my wing as she did not speak a word of Italian or French. It was here that I realised that this large, powerful, and superbly focused voice was something quite exceptional. She could, for example, have been a great Wagnerian, in the Florence Austral mould, but she was quite content to marry and accept a family life. She once confided that she doubted whether she would 'have kept her feet on the ground' had she encountered fame and fortune. She is, of course, far from being alone: there are countless people who have been more than adequately gifted but who lack the courage, perhaps foolhardiness, to take on a singing career. Nan was quite content to teach. During the late 1930s and early 40s Nan had a most promising pianist who would play for the more advanced pupils. Her name was Kathleen Ferrier.

If there is one singer above all others about whom I am constantly questioned it is Kathleen. Even thirty years after her death the very inflection in the mention of her name is invariably tinged with a deep and genuine affection and more than a hint of sadness. It is not just because she enjoyed such a short professional career, which nevertheless did not prevent her from becoming an

acclaimed international star, or simply admiration for the coura-
geous manner in which she fought cancer during her last few
precious years of life. No, it is something quite impossible to
define but which is inextricably part and parcel of that very special
magic she possessed and which became evident from the very
moment she opened her mouth to sing.

By some extraordinary coincidence I appeared with her from
her earliest days as a singer and was with her almost to the end:
in most instances the work was *Messiah*. I first heard reports of
Kathleen via Nan Chadwick for, as previously mentioned, Kathleen was an accomplished pianist and frequently played for Nan's
teaching in Blackburn. But woe betide Nan if her lessons went
beyond the appointed hour for Kathleen's father, a keen member
of the Salvation Army, would commence pacing up and down
outside the house anxiously awaiting his daughter's appearance.
After entering numerous piano competitions Kathleen eventually
gained enough confidence to compete as a singer and so impressed
the influential teacher of singing, Dr Hutchinson, at one meeting
that he instantly took Kathleen as a pupil. It was during these
hesitant first steps that I remember her, though according to
Charles Rigby's book on Kathleen she accompanied me at a BBC
broadcast from Manchester as early as 1933. I have to confess to
having no memory of this occasion. As singers we first met at a
Messiah at Lytham St Annes in December 1941 conducted by
Alfred Barker, the leader of the Hallé Orchestra. It was Kathleen's first *Messiah* after she had left Dr Hutchinson's devoted care
and attention. We shared a dressing room and when we came off
the platform Kathleen put down her score and said in a triumphant
yet relieved tone, 'Well Isobel, that's my first *real Messiah*!' My
reply did not require any degree of foresight: 'Well dear, you had
better start counting for it certainly won't be your last!'

For a while our paths crossed frequently. We met at Chorley
shortly afterwards for another *Messiah* and a little later there was
a 'lightweight' *Messiah* at Wolverhampton conducted by Dr Percy
Young. Kathleen especially relished singing *Oh thou that tellest*
with an 'authentic' accompaniment. During *He shall feed his flock*
she was also particularly taken by the way our voices blended
together and when we came off stage she could hardly contain
herself. 'Oh I love singing duets with you!' 'Thank you kindly',
I replied, 'perhaps we might sing some more in the not too distant
future', little realising that just a few years later we were actually

'I took part in a school pageant, a true Empire Day extravaganza, called *Britannia*. All the colonies were represented by their varied costumes and I played Britannia, singing something suitably patriotic'

Above: 'I won a scholarship to the High School in Dover Street, now Manchester High School'

Right: 'After the First World War we used to visit hospitals and camps together where we would sing to the wounded'

Left: 'I only discovered what to wear and what not to wear by watching other artists in my early years'

Right: 'I made my very first broadcast from Trafford Park in Manchester in the days before there was even a BBC! The broadcast took the form of a ballad concert with husband Harry contributing the "comic songs" and myself the other vocal items. Jo Lamb provided some violin solos whilst the versatile accompanist and occasional piano soloist was John Wills'

Above: Sir Henry Wood. 'He was always unfailingly kind and regardful for his singers'

Left: Hamilton Harty (shown here c. 1933 with the Principal Horn of the Hollywood Bowl Symphony Orchestra, Vincent de Rubertis) took a personal interest in every member of his orchestra

Left: 'It was during my long association with the Three Choirs Festival that I encountered most of the composers with whom I have worked'

Gladys Ripley was 'a very fun-loving girl who lived life to the full', and Heddle Nash 'always a joy to sing with'

'I had the honour of being the first British singer ever to perform at the Hollywood Bowl. It was quite a superb setting, an absolutely natural amphitheatre with a seating capacity of twenty-five thousand'

Portrait of the late 1940's

'I awoke with quite a spectacular black eye and had to spend some considerable time in the "make-up department". One has to look one's best when appearing on the stage of the Royal Albert Hall, even more so when my colleagues were, on this occasion, Laurence Olivier and Peggy Ashcroft' [during the Second World War; Roy Henderson is seated on the author's right]

'We took *Faust* to sixteen New Zealand towns and cities. The eventual Mefistofeles was Raymond Beatty, at that time one of Australia's principal basses. Heddle, of course, was my handsome Faust' [1940]

'One night the company was favoured by the unexpected appearance of Sir Thomas Beecham who, *en route* to Australia, learned of our presence and failed to resist the opportunity to conduct one of his all-time favourites'

'In 1953 I left the United Kingdom once more, this time for a recital tour of South Africa. I flew by the then much heralded Comet'

1978: with the insignia of the DBE

to record together duets by Purcell and Mendelssohn. These came about under unusual circumstances. It was, for Kathleen, the only honourable way she could complete her contract with Columbia after having had a contretemps with Walter Legge, then in charge of Columbia's classical recordings, who had obviously upset her during one of the earlier sessions. As she was most reluctant to record 'valuable' solo arias she compromised by offering duets with me. Poor Walter, he did not *always* win his battles!

Fate brought us together again during other peaks in her career and the work in question was invariably *Messiah*. I sang with her at her first London performance which took place in Westminster Abbey in May 1943; our gentlemen partners were Peter Pears and William Parsons and the performance was conducted by Reginald Jacques. Possibly more critical for the Northern lass was her first Hallé *Messiah*, in December 1945. Again, like some protective mother hen, I was by her side at the King's Hall in Belle Vue. Sir Malcolm Sargent conducted and this time Peter Pears was joined by Norman Walker. With the war over her international career rapidly blossomed and we met only infrequently though I was with her during her last *Messiah* at the Royal Albert Hall. She had by now been transported to the world of Mahler via the wings of Bruno Walter's chariot and was tackling with fearless courage contemporary opera – she was to make her operatic début in the world première of Britten's *The Rape of Lucretia* – but as a special concession to the Royal Choral Society she agreed to sing a further *Messiah*. There was a deep and inexpressible poignancy about that occasion.

Like any truly great artist Kathleen was, on rare instances, capable of fire and temperament. This would erupt only as a result of conduct – by herself as well as others – which she considered unprofessional. Otherwise the fire burning within her was always kept firmly under control; she was, despite her very few years as a singer, an out and out professional, utterly reliable, an exceptional musician and a wonderful companion. Even when things were against her it would be difficult to tell. For example, only her closest confidants were ever aware of the continued unhappiness she felt as a result of her short-lived marriage. Such problems would invariably be made light of as when I gently teased her about the attentions she was receiving from a most pleasant and charming fellow. 'Well Kathleen, are you going to marry him?', I mischievously enquired. 'Oh no!', came the reply, 'not for a long while. There's going to be a rehearsal next time!'

This was very typical of Kathleen's direct, honest approach to life. She did, in fact, possess an extraordinary zest for living, displaying an exceptional interest in all that surrounded her. I will always treasure the time we sang together in Bach's B minor Mass at King's College Chapel, Cambridge. After rehearsal Kathleen enquired if I would be wearing a hat for the performance. I informed her that indeed I would, I had always worn a hat for performances held in church. Kathleen nodded understandingly but said nothing. During the few hours' break before the performance she was nowhere to be found. Just as I began to wonder if she had come to any harm a gleeful Kathleen burst upon the scene exclaiming, 'How do you like it? I've bought a beany!' There she stood, as pleased as punch, wearing the latest line in millinery.

It was natural that some contraltos and mezzo-sopranos felt more than a twinge of jealousy at the astounding speed and success that came Kathleen's way. After all, she did not make her London début until 1943 yet had reached the absolute heights within five years. Lesser mortals had served a long and frequently arduous apprenticeship, and had struggled to build up their careers only to find themselves overtaken by this 'newcomer'. But as Parry Jones once remarked to me, 'We have not had a voice like this for a hundred years.' Kathleen was indeed very different and very special.

A contralto with whom I sang much more frequently, for our paths covered similar terrain, and with whom I became very closely acquainted, was Gladys Ripley. Her story has an uncanny parallel with that of Kathleen's for she too commenced her musical career as a pianist and was to be struck down by cancer at the very pinnacle of her career. As a vocalist Gladys appeared to be largely self-taught and, unlike Kathleen, began singing professionally at a very early age. Gladys was only seventeen when she made her first appearance at the Royal Albert Hall in a performance of *Elijah* conducted by Albert Coates, and her broadcast from Savoy Hill followed just two years later.

Gladys had not only a very remarkable voice – warm and flexible, it was a true contralto and very feminine – she was also a beautiful woman. She should have made a marvellous Carmen though I remember Heddle Nash saying, with considerable regret in his voice, that Gladys did not quite live up to expectations as a stage actress. She was a very fun-loving girl who lived life to the full. Her great sense of humour remained unimpaired through the many upsets she encountered in her short life, even during her brave fight against ill health, a battle eventually lost in 1955. I was immensely proud to serve along with Norman Allin, Robert Easton and Eric Greene on the committee of the Incorporated Society of Musicians which organised her memorial service in February 1956 at London's Church of St Sepulchre at Holborn Viaduct, where Sir Henry Wood is buried. And so it was that Gladys became just another name in that now famous Book of Remembrance which resides at the Musicians' Chapel at St Sepulchre. Her recordings, however, are a constant reminder of her art.

Of the contraltos who were pre-eminent among the generation before Kathleen and Gladys I knew Muriel Brunskill and Mary Jarred best. Muriel, a pupil of Blanche Marchesi, not only possessed a quite remarkable voice but also had the ability to adjust its scale and proportions to whatever she sang, be it opera, oratorio, Lieder, musicals, films or Gilbert and Sullivan. On stage she had an imposing presence and I will never forget seeing her as a superb Delilah in Manchester. She appeared born for the stage – small wonder that she joined the British National Opera Company in 1921 just one year after her début in this country. But she was also an imaginative Lieder singer, her early studies in Germany here paying obvious and handsome dividends.

I did not meet Mary Jarred until much later. Like myself she had served her apprenticeship in the North before venturing to London, where she studied with Victor Beigel, the teacher of Gervase Elwes and Lauritz Melchior. Although she went straight to Covent Garden immediately after these studies Melchior recommended that the Hamburg State Opera should employ her and it was here that she first made her very impressionable mark, singing much modern music, including Pfitzner and Berg. The emergence of the Nazis brought her back to England in the mid-1930s and it was then that I first met her, mainly in oratorio work, another genre which suited her admirably. It did not appear to be all that long after her return, though I suppose it must have been in the early 1950s, that she suddenly chose to retire. I was so surprised that I simply had to ask her why. 'Well', she explained referring to her voice, 'some days it's all right and some days it isn't.' A characteristic reply from a very modest person.

Astra Desmond, another Blanche Marchesi pupil, was also part of the fabric of music-making during the 1920s and 30s. Her musical sympathies were extremely broad, from ballad concerts to the songs of Kilpinen and Stravinsky, though she will undoubtedly be best remembered for her performances of Elgar. She sang, to high acclaim, all the great Elgarian contralto roles under his baton and became a close family friend of the composer. She was also a gifted linguist and translated many songs. We generally met at the Three Choirs Festival where, on one occasion when we arrived to rehearse just after the Second World War, she pounced on Harold Williams and declared in an off-hand manner as she first faced him, 'Oh, you've decided to come back have you?', a rather unfair jibe considering the amount of work he did throughout Australia and elsewhere during those troubled years. But Harold was not one to hold a grudge and the incident was soon forgotten. And we are *all* human: I can remember being jealous of Astra when she sang Marguerite in Berlioz's *Damnation of Faust* at a Leeds Festival, a role I very much coveted. This was another Berlioz work I had both sung and studied with Hamilton Harty. He took great pains to demonstrate that Berlioz wrote Marguerite for a soprano rather than a contralto. 'Marguerite', he explained, 'was a young girl and the mezzo range is only employed simply to heighten and "point" moments of sadness.'

I am hardly in a position to discuss the work and merits of my fellow sopranos for I rarely shared the same platform or programme with them, though I did see one of my close contemporaries, Dora Labbette, through many stages of her career. I first saw her from afar in the 1920s at such engagements as the Saturday afternoon ballad concerts. These meetings basically promoted publishers' new material; most singers of my generation have unveiled countless songs and ballads of varying degrees of triviality at these concerts. I admired Dora not only for her singing but also for the way she looked, always so elegantly dressed and always so beautiful!

When, in 1935 and aided by Sir Thomas Beecham, she was furtively transformed into a newly 'discovered' soprano 'Lisa Perli', Dora at last broke the chains of her reputation as an oratorio and concert singer by which she felt constricted and limited. Her subsequent stage successes were such that she seemed the ideal person to contact when I realised that an appearance as Marguerite in Gounod's *Faust* while on tour in New Zealand was more or less inevitable. I visited her in a house in St John's Wood, London, where she was preoccupied with some war work. We grabbed a quiet corner with the score in front of us and Dora gave me an idea of what stage actions I should attempt.

Tenors are supposed to be a temperamental and difficult breed, even more so than sopranos, but the tenor with whom I sang the most revealed no signs of such feckless display. He was, of course, Heddle Nash who was always a joy to sing with not simply because we personally got on so well together but also because his singing always afforded me the greatest delight. I would, for example, stand in the wings every night to hear him essay his great arias in *Faust* during our tour together in New Zealand.

I first heard the unusual name of Heddle Nash in Milan when some of my fellow students asked if I knew of him. After admitting that I did not they gleefully told me how, during an appearance as Canio in *Pagliacci* at the Carcano Theatre in Milan (incidentally, Heddle had made his operatic début here a short while previously as Almaviva in Rossini's *The Barber of Seville*), he had apparently used a whip on some other member of the cast. Whilst this was in accordance of the stage directions Heddle had, it appeared, scared everyone to death by displaying far more abandon than even the most temperamental Italian. All this made me most anxious to meet him and hear him sing. When I returned to England it was not long before such a meeting took place! I was astonished to discover a handsome man with riveting brown eyes and a gentle manner. It was not until a while later, after many concerts together, that I really came to know him well and appreciate his utter dedication to the art of singing.

He was a born singer and the beautiful effects which he obtained in such works as *The Dream of Gerontius, Messiah* and *The Creation* were, I felt, quite instinctive. One Three Choirs Festival performance of *Gerontius* will stay with me all my life. I sat in the back stalls, the entire length of the cathedral away, and heard a truly inspired performance. I have only to close my eyes to hear his highly individual voice ringing out in *Sanctis fortis* or achieving an exquisite *pianissimo* in *I went to sleep*. His recording of *Gerontius* should be studied by all students of singing. His was a unique voice and what he did with it was quite marvellous. He will, however, probably be best remembered for his operatic roles.

Although he was a born Mozartian his David in *Die Meistersinger* was quite out of this world: I do not ever recall seeing or hearing a more beautiful portrayal of this role. His actions were so convincingly boyish, a remarkable contrast to the stillness and repose he achieved when on the oratorio platform. There is a story that Heddle actually waylaid Toscanini in the street informing the Maestro that he was the best David Toscanini could ever have – and he got the job! He was, as I was to know from first hand experience, a splendid *Faust*, a role he sang in his first season at the Old Vic in 1925.

Although he was a serious artist Heddle's sense of humour was charming. He once told an engaging little story against himself. We were discussing 'fans' and the odd things they say and do from time to time when he recalled an incident which occurred one night after singing *Faust* at Sadler's Wells during the early days of his career. As usual he caught the last bus home (in those days a taxi was financially out of the question) which was, he explained, 'very full. I had to stand. Sitting below me were three girls who had evidently been to the performance. Said one, "Didn't you just love Heddle Nash?" to which the second replied "Oh yes, he was wonderful!" This, it seemed, was too much for the third who said in a bored, knowing voice, "My dears, have you met him?" adding after a pregnant pause, "*So* disappointing!" ' I for one can honestly say that Heddle did not once disappoint me in anything he did or sang throughout his glorious career.

Naturally I also sang with Heddle's more 'dramatic' colleagues, the most celebrated pair being Parry Jones and Walter Widdop. Parry was another great Wagnerian though naturally he excelled in the more dramatic roles. He spent the earliest years of his career in America where he had a high old time, singing almost anything which came to hand, be it ballad or opera. This was to stand him in good stead for, unlike so many of his kind, he had an extraordinary musical intelligence which enabled him to sing the most complicated score at almost a moment's notice. Besides his vast operatic repertoire, over ninety oratorios were apparently familiar to him. He was also naturally at ease in contemporary music, whether the first ever recording of Stravinsky's *Les Noces* which he recorded (with Roy Henderson also among the cast) under the composer's baton in 1934, or the first performance in this country of such disparate works as *Wozzeck, Mathis der Maler*, and *Doktor*

Faust. But he will always be remembered for his operatic performances, for opera appeared to be his life blood. When he
returned from his American jaunt, surviving the torpedoing of
the *Lusitania* en route, he joined first the Beecham Opera Company, then the D'Oyly Carte Opera and, after service in the First
World War, the Carl Rosa and British National Opera Companies. Four opera companies by the age of thirty-one! Such an
impressive list guarantees his abilities as a fine singing actor
though I cannot honestly say that his voice personally 'touched
me'. It was, for my ears, rather muscular and did not always
blend well with those around him, yet at the same time I must
add that he gave some of the best Wagner performances I have
ever heard; his Lohengrin in particular was justly famous.

Walter Widdop was another acclaimed Lohengrin. He in fact
sang Lohengrin's farewell at the Royal Albert Hall on the night
before his sudden death. When we first met, however, it was in
oratorio, though we later frequently teamed up at local concerts.
One night after such a concert Walter appeared particularly anxious to get away. When I asked why he explained that he was
going South the following day in order to audition for the British
National Opera Company. I wished him good luck though added
that I didn't envy him. He smiled, gave me a very old fashioned
look and said, 'Ah, but you will do!' Then off he went into the
night to commence his very considerable operatic career, not only
in this country but also in Europe.

Much later in my career I encountered many gifted tenors of
a younger generation. One who had a particularly attractive lyric
voice was David Lloyd. I frequently sang in duet with him, the
love duet from *La Bohème* always one of our most popular successes. His greatest attribute was his ability to spin a *bel canto* line,
made possible in his case by quite remarkable breath control. His
career was unfortunately dogged by bad luck. He made a notable
Glyndebourne début in 1938, but the Second World War
seriously interrupted his career, and it was later brought to a
premature end by a serious accident.

Then there was James Johnston, the tenor in the recordings I
made with Malcolm Sargent of *Messiah* and *Elijah* in the late
1940s. He had a good lyric voice but was not always, to my ear,
quite sure about what he should do with it. He triumphed chiefly
in opera both at Sadler's Wells and later at Covent Garden though
he also appeared frequently in oratorio. Then in the late 1950s he

71

returned to his native Belfast, disappearing as abruptly as he had first appeared.

Mention must also be made of William Herbert who was active in this country for only a few years, principally in the late 1940s and early 50s. His was a highly pleasing tenor voice and our work together in preparing Herbert Howells's *Hymnus paradisi* was an immense pleasure. He left for Australia not long after this and sadly died there shortly after his arrival. I also sang with Richard Lewis at the start of his career though this took place much earlier than I had first thought. He was born in Manchester of Welsh parents – a highly promising start to a vocal career! I found myself sharing the platform with him at a Leeds Festival, and was very impressed by this 'newcomer'. Then he informed me that he had sung with me years previously when he, a small treble, had sung the role of the youth in *Elijah*. I then quickly recalled the performance and my chagrin at being denied the opportunity of singing that part, something I looked forward to at every performance!

If I have shared the concert and oratorio platform with one singer above all others it must undoubtedly be with the baritone Harold Williams. The story goes that during his late teens in his native Australia he could not decide between a career as a cricketer or singer and that he allowed the toss of a coin to decide his fate. How grateful we must all be that the gods favoured singing. I thought Harold had no equal as Elijah because of his outstanding ability to get inside the character he portrayed, while to hear him sing Elgar's *The Kingdom* or *The Apostles* invariably reduced me to tears, such was the beauty of his singing. I will never forget the way he interpreted the recitative *I have prayed for thee that my faith fail not; and thou, when thou art converted, strengthen thy brethren* from *The Kingdom*. Musically it is a simple line but the extraordinary feeling Harold put into this brief passage was symptomatic of a very great musician. The voice itself was superbly even with a bright, burnished quality and the unforced clarity of his diction left one breathless. But what always made his performances so compelling was his phrasing, so ardent, so lyrical, yet always so stylish. Positive characterisation in oratorio is, I feel, so praiseworthy where the singer, denied costume and opportunity to act, has to convey a vast gamut of emotions only via the voice. Harold once surprised me when he admitted that he found oratorio more difficult than opera owing to the lack of external props of any kind. This was never apparent in any of his performances. Naturally, his operatic portrayals were equally convincing, particularly his scheming Iago to Frank Mullings's Otello. He was also an authoritative Boris Godunov and a villainous Mefistopheles, both of which he sang at Covent Garden. That rare ability of his to get right inside the character here stood him in very good stead.

Harold returned to Australia in the early 1950s to become professor of singing at the New South Wales Conservatory. He apparently continued to sing in public until well into his eighties although he sadly ended his days in a hostel for men. After his death a friend of mine told me that he had visited Harold at the home only to discover him in distressing circumstances. Had I known earlier I would have tried my utmost to have visited him for we really were such good friends.

Mention of *Elijah* will, of course, revive memories of Horace Stevens, for many the Elijah of his generation. I was very young when I first performed in *Elijah* with him. This was at Heckmondwike in Yorkshire, and he was inclined to be rather 'upstage', no doubt wondering who and what this little local soprano would be like! When the time came for us to rehearse the duet between Elijah and the widow he leaned across from his side and said rather haughtily, 'I suppose you've sung this before!', I thought this rather rude but politely replied, 'Oh yes, Mr Stevens.' When it came to the actual performance he stood up to sing without his score. I didn't allow this to affect the way I always sang and so held the score securely in front of me, though naturally having no need or cause to make reference to it. But when we came to our duet together I emulated Mr Stevens and placed my score on my seat. After the performance he apologised for his presumption. For all this he was a splendid Elijah, looking, with his full head of white hair, so patrician and benevolent.

Roy Henderson was yet another noted Elijah. I sang with him on many occasions in all kinds of repertoire, though we were never to become close friends. I first heard his voice via my little cat's whisker wireless and was full of admiration for his singing; it was a voice which seemed to broadcast particularly well. When I realised I was to sing with him in a Yorkshire *Messiah* I was both thrilled and excited. We were even staying at the same hotel and so we could talk endlessly about singing. I was, however, in for a great surprise as all he wanted to do was to discuss his newly acquired wife! His voice was a modest one, possessing neither the extremes of power nor of range, but it was employed with considerable taste and discrimination. He first came to prominence when he stepped in as a last minute replacement to take the demanding baritone part in Delius's *Mass of Life* at the Queen's Hall where, to everyone's amazement, he sang from memory. In oratorio Roy favoured the works of Elgar and Vaughan Williams to those of Handel and Haydn while in opera he also made a notable contribution, particularly during the early days of Glyndebourne. I met him most at concert engagements. It was at one such meeting at Grimsby that he considerably surprised me by producing a little pan pipe which he employed while singing Papageno's Act 1 aria from *The Magic Flute*. He also went to great pains to introduce each item in his programme. I am afraid I did not and still do not hold with such gimmicks. Explaining everything to everybody is, I believe, quite unnecessary. If the message in the song cannot be conveyed via one's singing then one should not be singing! At one stage Gerald Moore initiated a similar move and I think I offended him rather badly when I refused at a recital in Ilkley to let him introduce my songs. Singing one's repertoire in English, a constant crusade of mine, was surely more than enough. I have always strongly believed that I should sing wherever possible in the vernacular. Once in America I was interviewed by a reporter on one of the big newspapers and caused quite a controversy when they quoted my beliefs that the best manner of singing opera was to sing it in English so that everyone would understand.

If ever there were a classic example of a singer being ruled from the head rather than the heart – and who can say which is the preferable approach? – it was Keith Falkner, a man of keen intelligence. I loved his singing of Bach. The fastidiousness of his overall approach allied to the spirituality of Bach's music, particularly in such works as the B minor Mass, was completely appropriate. In such roles as Elijah, however, Keith appeared reluctant to let himself go in a somewhat operatic manner, something which I feel this score requires. This undoubtedly also explains Keith's dislike of Elgar's *Dream of Gerontius*, the part of Gerontius surely being as operatic as anything written by Verdi and Puccini. Despite this Keith possessed a marked sympathy for Vaughan Williams - demonstrated in a chilling performance I once heard of *The new ghost* – as well as Butterworth and Somervell whose Housman settings he so memorably recorded.

I sometimes used to get mad with him when I felt he was being over-careful with himself. I once recall having completed a concert together when he decided that his throat 'didn't feel good' and that he would therefore have to cancel an *Elijah* due to be performed somewhere the next day. I told him that his throat certainly sounded all right on stage that night and that it was sure to be all right the following day. So he went and did his *Elijah* and an audience was not disappointed. Sometimes we singers only require just a few words of encouragement!

There are so many names, so many friends and acquaintances, that it is naturally impossible to recall all of them here, but mention of baritones would not be complete without Henry Cummings whose singing I always recall with affection. He was another all-rounder, equally at home on the operatic stage as the concert platform, who had a remarkably varied repertoire which, I was pleased to note, included Harty's *Mystic trumpeter*. Henry was, in the best sense of the word, a tasteful singer, very careful for his art. He continued the British tradition of John Coates, Robert Radford and Henry Plunket Greene, all of whom were his tutors at various times. His gifts were later approached by Richard Standen whose voice greatly impressed me on account of its special warmth. His work was always scrupulously prepared and, as a result, he always gave a superb performance.

Finally I must make mention of some of those indispensable gentlemen who provide the necessary foundation of any vocal ensemble, the basses. How paradoxical that audiences thrill to the basso profundo's low notes almost as much as to the coloratura soprano's stratospheric squeaks. One could, for example, see an audience literally sliding towards the edge of their seats in anticipation when a bass such as Robert Easton would descend to his low notes in a work such as *The Creation*. Bob's big break came late after a long but finally invaluable apprenticeship in 1929 when he deputised for Harold Williams at a Crystal Palace performance of *Messiah* conducted by Beecham. Later, of course, came 'Branny', Northumberland's very own Owen Brannigan who not only popularised the songs of his native country but created so many roles in Britten's stage works: Swallow in *Peter Grimes*, Noye in *Noye's Fludde* and Bottom in *A Midsummer Night's Dream*. Although we did not meet as often as I would have wished I warmed to his splendidly bluff Northern manner and we always got on well. Norman Walker will also never be forgotten. He was another who fought ill health during the last years of his far too brief career, a man of considerable courage. I well remember the last time I ever sang with him. It was at the Central Hall, Westminster, after he had suffered a stroke and was valiantly battling on complete with stick; his voice, though, was quite unimpaired. For all the comparative brevity of his career it was remarkably varied, ranging from appearances during his early years in several films, including *Sing as We Go* with Gracie Fields, to imposing portrayals, notably King Mark in *Tristan und Isolde* at Covent Garden.

If there was a bass, however, who dominated the entire British scene in my day it was the marvellous Norman Allin. What a remarkable voice he had, beautifully even and sonorous, exceptionally flexible for a true basso (his runs were out of this world), and as with so many of his contemporaries, his enunciation was faultless. Surprisingly he lacked self-confidence. There is a line in *Messiah*, 'The Kings of the earth rise up', which leaps to a top E and which for him, a true bass, was rather high. It used to worry him terribly. I always used to try and reassure him; at every performance we sang together I would say 'It doesn't matter Norman, just throw it away', but it made no difference. Then in 1932, still upon the heights, he vowed he would never sing *Messiah* again. All part of the tribulations of being a perfectionist. Yet many things he sang incomparably, for example Sarastro's aria *Within this hallowed dwelling* from Mozart's *The Magic Flute*.

We first met at a concert in Oldham when I discovered him standing in the wings listening to me. After that our paths crossed frequently, not only in oratorio work but also in concerts where we made a speciality of the Act 2 duet from *The Seraglio* between Blonde and Osmin, *I leave you, but bid you beware*. Lancashire born, he was tall and well built as befits a man with a 'bottom D'. He was always a very kind and genuine person who, like Harold Williams, sadly spent his final years in a home, though in far happier surroundings, the superb Musicians' Benevolent Home in Hereford. I would try and visit him as often as I could as he was always grateful to receive a visitor.

Sir Henry Wood hit the nail on the head when he wrote of Norman in his autobiography *My Life of Music*:

I have always thought it a pity that Allin is of such a retiring disposition for, had he cared, he might have become one of the world's finest operatic basses. I believe his operatic roles number fifty. I imagine he loved the English countryside and his home too well, and who can blame him?

Norman was indeed a very simple and unambitious man who devoted his entire energies to perfecting his art.

CHAPTER SEVEN

Composer Collaborations

THE oratorios of Bach, Handel and Haydn have naturally formed the backbone of my repertoire. It has also been my privilege to perform many new works under the guidance of the composer, some of whom have been among the most pre-eminent of their day.

My very first encounter with a composer of any kind stems from my early years in Manchester when I befriended Eric Fogg, son of my teacher Madam Sadler-Fogg and Charles Fogg, that purveyor of so much indispensable knowledge. Musically Eric and I grew up rather like brother and sister and this no doubt blinded me to the full extent of his quite exceptional gifts. He had, for example, made quite a stir when, at Henry Wood's express invitation and aged only seventeen, he conducted his own ballet suite *The Golden Butterfly* at a 1920 Promenade concert. The following year was an auspicious one for both of us: in the February *The Golden Butterfly* received its Hallé première and in the following November I made my Hallé début. Eric later took several BBC appointments: he became familiar to countless children as 'Uncle Eric' in the BBC North Region *Children's Hour* and was later appointed conductor of the Empire Orchestra. His tragic death at the age of thirty-six in 1939 deprived this country of a musician of outstanding promise.

As a composer I knew Eric principally as the author of some charming and exquisite songs, which I was pleased to include in my recitals long after his death. One of the most beautiful was *Peace*, which was even taken up and recorded by Dame Clara Butt. When I hear this record I still feel a little piqued as it was a work I too would have given much to have recorded as it always made a great impact on one's audience. But so did *Spindrift* and *One morning in a flower garden*; like the best of his songs, they are of instant appeal and perfectly crafted. Though undoubtedly compositions of the old school and far removed from the avant-garde they were also much more than trivial ballads and made considerable technical and interpretative demands of the singer.

Eric had a delightful outgoing disposition and playful sense of humour, something which always came to mind whenever I sang Granados's *The maiden and the nightingale* with him. He would do his utmost, generally in rehearsal but occasionally (such was his daring) during a performance, to put me off that final high, sustained note, perhaps by an obvious alien chord or some subtle change of tempo. I must, however, emphasise that in all other respects he was a quite splendid accompanist and always a joy to work with.

If singing with Eric proved to be my first working relationship with a real live composer I was in no way in awe of him – I had known him far too long! No, my first encounter with a composer of stature and repute (and what a reputation) was with the indomitable figure of Dame Ethel Smyth, that passionate and unswerving champion of women's rights. Sadly her music is now little regarded though in her day, during the early decades of this century, she was a highly influential celebrity in British music. Even a conductor of Bruno Walter's stature felt compelled to mention in his autobiography that Ethel Smyth was 'a composer of quite special significance who is certain of a permanent place in musical history'. If that place is currently unclear it seemed abundantly evident in the 1920s. Both she and her music were very much part of the 'modern' scene and my considerable surprise can therefore be imagined when I received an approach from Sir Henry Wood to perform two songs from Dame Ethel's opera, *The Wreckers*. Despite my Hallé début in Casella's *The Venetian Convent*, I was far from being known as an interpreter of modern music. Why Dame Ethel should have specifically asked for me I was never to know, particularly as there was at that time a soprano who had made a considerable name for herself by singing contemporary music. In fact she must have felt that she had cornered the 'contemporary market' for I was later told that she was more than a little irked that I should have been asked to perform these songs: 'Bella Baillie's going to do them', she apparently said with great indignation, 'someone from *Manchester*!' as if that was the final insult. I did not, however, let it bother me. I viewed it simply as another interesting and unusual task, a further string to my bow though I have to admit that I do not think the songs suited me particularly well. As with everything else I sang I naturally attempted to do my best even if I found the songs far from easy to sing, particularly that which commenced 'Ha! ha! ha! the rats in sight!', though it was easy to understand why *The Wreckers* had a great vogue despite its disastrous Leipzig première in 1906 (it was only after Sir Thomas Beecham's persuasive direction at His Majesty's Theatre in 1909 that the opera became something of a hit). Naturally I was considerably assisted by Sir Henry who was proud to write in his autobiography *My Life of Music*, 'I must have played practically everything Dame Ethel has written.' During the final rehearsal Dame Ethel sat and listened most attentively but did not interject in any way, such was her reliance upon and confidence in Sir Henry. She knew that if any corrections were necessary he would tell me.

The day after the performance at the Queen's Hall, the very hall in which Nikisch had conducted a concert performance of the opera in 1908 with Blanche Marchesi and John Coates in the principal roles, she wrote the following colourful and characteristic note from her home at Coign near Woking.

My dear Miss Baillie,

I didn't half thank you last night – in my anguish at perhaps missing the train & my haste to catch it (which I did). If I hadn't it wd have meant hanging around foodless at Waterloo till 11.50! I wish our songs hadn't come off on the saddest day of my life & one of the most deadly busy ones [She had buried her sister between rehearsal and concert time] I thought you sang them beautifully & had studied so carefully . . . a rock of strength! My only hope is that you get a nice press - I never want to know what they say of me, so never read it. In the WP (my paper) is a headline 'Dame E.S. as conductor' & thou' I read all the rest of the paper that column will not be so much as glanced at!!

Yours sincerely,
Ethel Smyth

Only a little while after this concert Dame Ethel began making tentative plans for me to repeat these songs in Germany with Furtwängler conducting, plans which did not, however, come to fruition. I was destined never to sing in Germany even after travelling there in the 1950s to sing a series of recitals organised by the Arts Council. While walking to my first rehearsal with Wainright Morgan, my accompanist, we were welcomed by a hit-and-run motorist and both brought back on stretchers!

I also once participated in Dame Ethel's Mass in D at the Royal Albert Hall with the composer conducting. She was an energetic conductor who drew commendable results. The Mass is an exceptionally beautiful work and one well worthy of revival. I remember how we all gathered together for rehearsals at the Royal College. Dame Ethel arrived in the nick of time and just a little flustered. She had, it transpired, been lunching with Lord and Lady Somebody-or-other and had found it difficult to extricate herself from the proceedings. Such was her determination not to be late for rehearsal that she appeared still clutching her napkin from the aristocratic table!

It was during my long association with the Three Choirs Festival that I encountered most of the composers with whom I have worked. My introduction to the Festival occurred as a result of the then rather puritanical views held by the committee. When it became known that an eminent Australian soprano engaged to sing at Worcester in 1929 was living with someone other than her husband her invitation was withdrawn and I was chosen as her replacement. I last sang at the Festival in 1955: a tally of eighteen Festivals, fifteen of them consecutive, during twenty-three Choirs meetings. After that 1955 gathering I received a most courteous letter from Dr Sumsion explaining that as there were so many young singers awaiting their Three Choirs Festival chance I was not going to receive an invitation to participate the following year. I accepted my congé!

Having spent so many years at the Festival it was inevitable that I should have enjoyed the frequently revealing and always rewarding experience of a composer's direction. Certain composers one met simply in passing, even so some made a considerable impact merely by their presence, Samuel Barber for example. When he was at Hereford in 1946 to attend a performance of his *Adagio for strings* he made a great artistic and personal impression on everyone. The astounding beauty of the setting from the slow

81

movement of his First String Quartet was almost as hypnotic as his strikingly handsome good looks.

But above all, of course, it was the towering figure of Sir Edward Elgar who dominated the Three Choirs Festival throughout the first three decades of this century. Under his baton I sang the great soprano roles in both *The Kingdom* and *The Apostles* as well as the equally moving, though now almost forgotten *For the fallen*, undeniably a patriotic, wartime work (it forms the third part of his oratorio *The Spirit of England*) which at one time used to be performed regularly on Armistice Day. This has been aptly described as 'the greatest musical war memorial' and its impact always made itself felt on both performers and audience. I well remember being so moved in one performance, particularly at the moment 'We will remember them', that I had great difficulty in singing, such is the work's heart-breaking emotion.

More familiar are Elgar's *The Apostles* and *The Kingdom*. In the earlier of these oratorios, *The Apostles*, first launched at the Birmingham Festival in 1903, Elgar employs an exceptionally large number of performers, two additional bass singers to the traditional quartet of soprano, contralto, tenor and bass, plus a particularly large orchestra. The soprano is allotted the roles of the Blessed Virgin and the Angel. *The Kingdom*, given its première by Hans Richter in 1906, again at Birmingham, is, by contrast, much more reflective and autumnal, quintessential Elgar as anyone who knows its most familiar section, the soprano's great *scena*, *The sun goeth down*, will surely readily agree. Elgar here reverts to the standard vocal quartet and a more traditional sized orchestra. The difference in the number of vocalists in these works reflects, I think, their contrasted differences: *The Apostles* is an ensemble work with much character portrayal, whereas *The Kingdom* contains a great series of magnificent solos.

Elgar was by no means a *great* conductor though he was certainly much more than adequate. He somehow managed to inspire the best of his musicians who, having placed themselves at his disposal, were intent on giving their all for a very great man. He relied a great deal on his singers, hardly ever correcting them but, in the precious hours of rehearsal before a performance, concentrating more on tidying up orchestral detail. I also sang with him at the Croydon Festival which during the 1920s and 30s proved to be the South-East's very own Elgar festival. It was at one of these festivals that he corrected me, the only occasion he ever did so. We were rehearsing for a performance of *The Kingdom* and when I came to the phrase 'The sword hath piercèd mine own heart' he stopped me and asked for a stronger emphasis on the word 'piercèd', requiring more stress on the first syllable.

Elgar knew much about singers and singing and I once quizzed him about Emma Albani who was such a prominent figure at the turn-of-the-century and who had sung with him on many occasions, not least in the première of *The Apostles*. I was particularly curious to learn something about her after I discovered that she did not sing *Messiah* complete, preferring to allocate some of the soprano solos to a second imported soprano. When I asked Elgar what her voice was like, he paused for a moment then smiled. 'It was a beautiful golden sound', he replied, then adding after further thought, 'but she didn't have your brains!' It was only much later that I discovered how characteristic this remark was when I read that Elgar wrote despairingly to a friend while casting around for suitable singers to participate in the first performance of *The Apostles*, 'Oh! these singers – *where* are their *brains?*'

Thoughts of the Three Choirs Festival naturally bring to mind Herbert Howells's *Hymnus paradisi*, a work of quite exceptional beauty the première of which I gave at Gloucester in 1950 with the tenor William Herbert and the composer conducting. *Hymnus paradisi*, a deeply reflective and personal requiem for Howells's son who died in childhood, begins and ends with part of the text from the *Mass for the dead*, yet for all its contemplative, meditative calm, the work is by no means morbid or sanctimonious. From the opening orchestral *Preludio* it captures that peculiar English mood of reflective melancholy. The work surprised many critics, for Herbert Howells was at that time considered to be more of a miniaturist and its instant success led to the work being repeated at the two subsequent festivals where, once again, I was able to luxuriate in the glorious soprano part.

Herbert was deeply touched by the work's immediate and sympathetic reception. After the first performance he wrote:

Dearest Isobel,

You know how I feel about your grand help in 'Hymnus Paradisi': but I want to tell you again in writing, in case my spoken word was feeble and indistinct. From first to last, in writing the soprano solo part, yours was the only voice I heard in my mind's ear. And to have you *actually* singing in the work was sheer bliss.

83

I don't deserve the luck having you and Bill Herbert at my side in the new work! Take care of yourself always. And bless you for all your help. Dorothy joins me in love to you.

Herbert

A few days later his wife Dorothy also took to paper.

My dear Isobel,

I'm jealous of Herbert's getting in first with a note to you: but I don't wonder at his being in a hurry to write, I know how much your lovely work in 'Hymnus Paradisi' delighted him and he certainly had always talked to me of 'Isobel's part' (meaning the soprano solo!).

I'm just as grateful as he is: and I think the success of the work that means so much to us (because of its link with that beloved son of ours) has put new heart into Herbert. Anyhow, your share in the success is so great that I, too, want to send you this little note of gratitude. And it was good to see you so much recovered from your dreadful experience in Germany [a reference to the afore-mentioned accident in Germany] – we were all so anxious about it when we heard of it. But you sing as if it had never happened!

I wish it had been possible to have had a talk with you apart (or rather away from) a crowd of people – but that is impossible at a Three Choirs Festival. Maybe sometime I shall get that opportunity.

My best wishes and thanks,
Yours affectionately,
Dorothy Howells

I later sang the work with other conductors, once in Salisbury Cathedral under a conductor whose ideas about the work appeared to depart radically from that established by the earlier performances with the composer and, more importantly, from that indicated by the score. He seemed in such a hurry, which proved particularly ruinous to movements like the *Requiem aeternam* and *The Lord is my shepherd*. I do not recall ever doing such a thing before or since but I was so indignant I simply had to stop him during rehearsal, exclaiming 'That's far too quick, Mr X.' His reply, 'We like it rather brisk!', stunned me. Herbert was sitting in the cathedral at the time but did not intervene - he is not the kind of person to engage in battle with anyone! Blushingly, I have to admit that I won in the end; I took my part at the pace I considered appropriate and the conductor was more or less forced to follow me. This runs contrary to my strict belief that the conductor is in overall charge and must have the unqualified respect of his singers. It was an isolated and, I feel, justified lapse on my part. For me a slow tempo for the *Requiem aeternam* was crucial. I settled upon it instinctively when I first prepared the score and it was an approach which was fully endorsed by the composer when we commenced orchestral rehearsals.

I first worked with Herbert at the 1931 Three Choirs Festival at Gloucester, a Wednesday Secular Concert at the Shire Hall, where I sang his suite of five songs for high voice and orchestra, *In green ways*. It was a quite extraordinary concert in that every work on the programme was conducted by the composer. In addition Vaughan Williams conducted *Job*, Elgar his *Nursery Suite* and Holst his arrangement of Bach's *Fugue à la gigue*.

Herbert and I always got along quite splendidly together. I would call him my 'pocket Adonis' for although he was short of stature he was quite perfectly proportioned and we would flirt quite mercilessly yet harmlessly over a cup of tea during a break in rehearsals or after a performance. Infrequently we worked together in recitals. I will, for example, always treasure the memory of our work together on a BBC recital devoted exclusively to the songs of Ivor Gurney broadcast in November 1946. We were both somewhat overcome by the extraordinary sadness of these songs which included *Desire in spring*, *You are my sky* and *Severn meadows*. I could hardly sing *Sleep* for the emotion which welled up inside me as a result of the quite potent combination of Gurney's music and John Fletcher's poem.

> Come sleep, and with thy sweet deceiving
> Lock me in delight a while;
> Let some pleasing dream beguile
> All my fancies; that from thence
> I may feel an influence
> All my powers of care bereaving!
> Though but a shadow, but a sliding.
> Let me know some little joy!
> We that suffer long annoy
> Are contented with a thought
> Through an idle fancy wrought:
> O let my joys have some abiding!

Before leaving the subject of the Three Choirs Festival for a while I must take this opportunity to mention that very special atmosphere which enhanced these meetings. Much of it was obviously because the concerts were given in cathedrals and during a time when there was never any applause. This is something I always preferred in such surroundings. One can always tell if an audience has enjoyed a work without having to hear a single clap; besides that indefinable rapport with one's audience one could also frequently hear a corporate, spontaneous sigh of pleasure. Of the three venues the comparatively small Hereford Cathedral was naturally the more intimate while Gloucester Cathedral proved the most impressive. During my association with the festivals Dr Sumsion was the sole director of events at Gloucester. At Hereford there was Sir Percy Hull, later succeeded by Meredith Davies, while at Worcester there was Sir Ivor Atkins, later succeeded by David Willcocks. Sir Ivor once left me high and dry on a top A during the phrase *How great are thy signs* in a performance of *The Kingdom*, an incident which proved to me that I possessed greater reserves of breath than I thought I had! It is so easily done and he is far from being alone – it simply lingers in the mind as it happened on a top A. Sir Ivor eventually brought the orchestra in otherwise I might still be there valiantly hanging on to my top note.

The plenitude of festivals which are so much part of today's musical life are by no means a recent phenomenon as will now be evident. One festival, however, which sadly seems to have faded away is the Winchester Festival which was long presided over by Sir George Dyson. Though a Yorkshireman by birth it is difficult to think of him being anything other than a Wykehamist for it was at Winchester, where he was Music Master at the College for thirteen years, that he instigated the annual festival and where he eventually died in 1965. George Dyson was a pupil of Stanford at the Royal College of Music and there are some remarkable parallels in their careers. Stanford was drawn to Chaucer's *Canterbury Tales* and penned an opera on the subject which was first produced at Drury Lane in 1884. Later, Dyson, also destined to become the Director of the Royal College of Music, grazed in the rich Chaucerian pastures, eventually writing his *The Canterbury Pilgrims*, subtitled *Portraits chosen from the Prologue*, in 1930. I had the considerable pleasure of participating in the première on 19 March 1931 with Steuart Wilson and Roy Henderson

86

with Sir George conducting. It was a strange and remarkable experience singing the work for the first time as the audience remained totally silent until after my second solo, a portrait of the Wife of Bath, when suddenly they burst into applause, something which brought a broad smile to Sir George's face. The score was quite unlike anything which I had sung before, particularly the Nun's extended solo with female chorus, though it was the 'naughtiness' of the Wife of Bath's solo which caught everyone's attention. Even Sir George confessed that he did not realise I had so much of the Wife of Bath in me! *The Canterbury Pilgrims* is a very engaging work though it needs to be heard several times before its full riches become evident. History has subsequently been rather hard on both Dyson and his music and he is now firmly branded as a dyed-in-the-wool conservative. True, conservatism is evident in *The Canterbury Pilgrims* but there are delightful moments of a simple, forthright humour as exemplified by *A good wife was there of beside Bath* and *There was a clerk of Oxenford*; the entire work also has a very individual and special quality, a perfectly judged twentieth-century English oratorio in an unusual pastoral vein.

In 1952 I had the pleasure of singing in another performance of *The Canterbury Pilgrims* at the Royal Albert Hall, again conducted by the composer. Before the performance Sir George reminded me that it was over thirty years since we had first performed the work. During the interval who should enter the green room but Steuart Wilson. I took the opportunity to remind him of the same fact. 'Just fancy', I said, 'It's more than thirty years since we sang together in the première.' Quick as a flash he replied, 'And by gosh, you'd better watch out, you're the only one left on your feet!' Only then did the full truth dawn, I *was* the only one of the three original soloists still singing professionally. That performance prompted a brief but kindly thank you from Sir George:

My dear Isobel,

    I must tell you how you surpassed even your inimitable self last Friday night. The best ever, and we *all* thought so.

                                    Affectionately,
                                      G.D.

Still on my feet, I also participated in an even later performance of *The Canterbury Pilgrims* given by the Winchester Music Club in February 1963 at the Guildhall in Winchester. The performance, with Edgar Fleet and Owen Brannigan as my colleagues, was directed by Christopher Cowan. The accompanying programme explained the reasoning behind the programme:

> In offering this performance as an affectionate tribute to the composer, who will celebrate his eightieth birthday this year, the Winchester Music Club wishes also to mention gratefully the work of Lady Dyson who prepared the Chaucerian text for modern use, and to Isobel Baillie, who first sang the Nun and the Wife of Bath and has given the keenest pleasure by her singing in the City on many other memorable occasions.

Sir George was genuinely delighted by this tribute.

I also participated in the première of Dyson's *Quo Vadis?* which not only suffered a delayed birth but a subsequent further gestation period. *Quo Vadis?* was scheduled to take place at the 1939 Three Choirs Festival at Hereford under the composer's baton with Astra Desmond, Heddle Nash and Roy Henderson. 'G.D.' contributed his own programme note in which he stated that 'the first five movements are offered as part one . . . and I propose to postpone the writing of part two until I can approach the task with a new perspective, both of its demands and of its end'. But all this was not to be as the entire festival was abandoned at the last minute due to the outbreak of the Second World War. When the Festival resumed in 1946 at Hereford *Quo Vadis?* was eventually given its première. There were two alterations from the original announcement: George Pizzey sang in place of Roy Henderson and the work was announced as *Quo Vadis?* Part 1. When repeated the following year at Gloucester Heddle and I were joined by Gladys Ripley and Norman Walker. Sir George was still experiencing difficulties with Part 2, for his programme note now stated 'Part two exists yet only in a further sequence of poems and some rough sketches of their musical treatment.'

I think it might have been at this 1947 performance that I gently castigated the unfortunate composer, pointing out that the soprano was alone in not having a solo movement. 'Ah!', came the mysterious reply, 'Just you wait until Part 2 is completed!' Sure enough in 1949 at the Hereford Festival the complete *Quo Vadis?* was unveiled. Heddle and I were rejoined by Astra Desmond and a new face to the Three Choirs Festival, Trevor Anthony. The composer, who naturally conducted, had, I discovered, remained true to his word – Part 2 opened with an extended and rewarding solo for soprano, *Dear stream! Dear bank! Where often I have sat.*

Sir George was a splendidly direct and uncomplicated person who was always highly professional to work with. Like so many musicians, though quite unlike myself, he was also a mathematician and technician. During the First World War he even wrote a *Manual of Grenade Fighting* which was officially adopted by the War Office – a far cry from the saucy music given to the Wife of Bath!

Another composer who enjoyed what can only be described as his own personal festival in his own town was Vaughan Williams whose Dorking Festival became one of the highlights of music-making in the Surrey and Sussex area. I sang under his direction at Dorking many times. If I am now unable to recall each and every one of those appearances the special concert celebrating Vaughan Williams's eightieth birthday remains an indelible memory. Sir Adrian Boult and William Cole shared the conducting and the works included *The hundredth psalm*, *The Oxford elegy*, the *Five mystical songs* and the *Benedicite*.

It was, I think, at the 1932 Worcester Three Choirs Festival that I first made Vaughan Williams's acquaintance, singing the *Benedicite*, then one of his newest and much-acclaimed pieces, in the same concert that I sang Elgar's *For the fallen*, also conducted by the composer. In that ill-fated 1939 Festival I was also due to sing Vaughan Williams's cantata *Dona nobis pacem* written three years earlier to commemorate the centenary of the Huddersfield Choral Society. How ironic that a performance of a work which was a powerful warning against the coming of war should itself be prevented by war. In 1946 with the restoration of peace we repeated the *Benedicite* at Hereford and in 1954 I sang my last Vaughan Williams at a Three Choirs Festival with a performance of the Pastoral Symphony at Worcester, again under VW's baton. On this instance the wordless cantilena, sung by the soprano out of sight from the side of the stage, was almost rendered inaudible by the ominous drone of several aircraft then still, it seemed, a reminder of war.

One Vaughan Williams memory crowds out all others, one that again proved to be close to the Second World War. It was in 1938 when I was invited to participate in *Serenade to Music*, a work 'composed', to quote Vaughan Williams's dedication in the score, 'for, and dedicated to, Sir Henry Wood on the occasion of his jubilee, in grateful recognition of his great services to music'. Sir Henry was never happier than when surrounded and working with singers and so he requested a jubilee piece for sixteen solo singers and orchestra. I was invited to be one of that team along with Stiles-Allen, Elsie Suddaby, Eva Turner, Margaret Balfour, Astra Desmond, Muriel Brunskill, Mary Jarred, Heddle Nash, Walter Widdop, Parry Jones, Frank Titterton, Roy Henderson, Robert Easton, Harold Williams and Norman Allin. The choice of text was from Shakespeare's *The Merchant of Venice*.

> How sweet the moonlight sleeps upon this bank.
> Here will we sit and let the sounds of music
> Creep in our ears; soft stillness and the night
> Become the touches of sweet harmony.

and it inspired one of Vaughan Williams's most magical and evocative compositions. It was also written with the individual vocal qualities of each singer in mind to the extent that Vaughan Williams indicated each singer's phrase by the insertion of their initials in the score. Perhaps this personal identification explains why the work does not have the same magic when performed by a quartet of singers or a small chorus, both alternatives endorsed by the composer. When we were first presented with the score I saw that after singing in consort, I had the awesome task of leading the sixteen solo contributions. I also have to confess that I looked askance when I saw my phrase 'of sweet harmony' – not only was it very exposed but it rose to a top A within two bars! It was truly an ordeal and I think I lost a deal of weight worrying about those three bars. Why Vaughan Williams thought I could do it I never knew. My colleagues knew how I felt and during rehearsals they would encourage me by a round of applause after I had sung my phrase. Although we were sixteen soloists all thrown in together, as it were, we all got along swimmingly. It was probably the first time I had met Eva Turner and Elsie Suddaby for our paths were unlikely to have crossed before. Vaughan Williams came, I think, only to the last rehearsal. Like Ethel Smyth he was content merely to sit and listen, leaving Sir Henry in total charge.

It had been hoped to hold the jubilee concert on St Cecilia's Day but Rachmaninov, the guest of honour and soloist in his own Second Piano Concerto, was only able to come from

America for just one day, 5 October 1938. He came especially for this one engagement and left for America the very next day. During the second half of the concert Rachmaninov sat in the box with Lady Wood and was, according to her book *The Last Years of Henry J. Wood*, 'moved to tears' when he heard the *Serenade to Music*. Sir Henry was also most pleased and wrote to the composer a sincere thank-you stating that the Serenade had raised 'his Jubilee Concert out of the ordinary rut and lent real distinction to Part 2'. The entire proceeds of the concert were paid into a fund for the endowment of beds in London hospitals for the benefit of orchestral musicians. I was instantly aware that this was a 'great occasion' and I think the reason that the singing had proved a success was that we had all been used to ensemble singing.

All sixteen of us reappeared in the *Serenade to Music* at a concert in the newly opened Royal Festival Hall in 1951. My one thought was not so much my opening phrase but whether the platform would withstand our combined weight. With few exceptions most of us were then near to the twelve stone mark and some noticeably more so!

Mention of the Festival Hall does bring back a disturbing memory of my first recital there. The acoustics were quite unlike anything I had previously encountered and I quite thought I had lost my voice. I could not hear myself and after the first section came off stage pouring with perspiration and in quite a state. But Gerald Moore, my accompanist, assured me that all was not as it appeared. The acoustics are, I think, most acceptable from the audience's vantage point but less so from the poor performer's.

I also worked with Vaughan Williams at the Promenade Concerts when he would frequently appear to conduct his own symphonies and where I sang in both his Sea Symphony and Pastoral Symphony. I also remember performances with him at the Edinburgh Festival and with the Hallé. Vaughan Williams was as kind and considerate a conductor as he was a person, perhaps too much so for his gentleness could be taken advantage of. I well recall a rehearsal of one of his works which was to be performed at Bromley. On completing my solo I noticed my 'gentleman' colleague who was due to sing only at the very end of the work sitting on the platform blatantly reading a newspaper. What an insult it seemed to me, revealing no respect for either the conductor or the composer, in this instance one and the same person!

Earlier mention of Rachmaninov's visit to Sir Henry Wood's

jubilee concert reminds me of the unforgettable experience I had when working with Rachmaninov in the preparation of a performance of his choral masterpiece *The Bells*. This was to be given under the baton of Sir Henry, who had first introduced the work in 1921, and in the presence of the composer, the climax of the 1936 Sheffield Festival. Sir Henry was not only a staunch advocate of Rachmaninov's music but also a lifelong friend of the composer, and Rachmaninov's presence at the jubilee concert was a public gesture of gratitude to his greatest English exponent. Rachmaninov even revised the choral writing of the third movement of *The Bells*, though this did not apparently prove especially irksome as the work was Rachmaninov's favourite.

I was first approached by Ibbs & Tillett, my agents, who asked if I would like to participate in the concert. When I readily agreed they first informed me that my vocal partners would be two long-standing friends, Parry Jones and Harold Williams, and then stipulated that I would have to travel to London in order to go through the soprano solo with the composer. It was with considerable exhilaration and not a little trepidation that I found myself entering the Piccadilly Hotel to meet the great man. Great man in all senses, for when I arrived at his suite he rose from a fireside chair and loomed taller and taller; it appeared as if he would never stop. Even more impressive than his slender height was his face, the most beautiful but also the saddest I think I have ever seen. Once the pleasantries of the introduction were over he went to the piano and handed me a score. I sang the solo in its entirety to his accompaniment; what a thrill! Its long languorous lines recalling the bells of marriage and bliss, with a considerable degree of melancholy so characteristic of the composer, are a God-given gift to any lyric soprano.

> Listen to the holy wedding bells
> Their melody tells of a world of happiness
> Like a pair of distant eyes
> They gaze through the quiet air of night

After this playthrough I took out my pencil in preparation for Rachmaninov's observations and qualifications but to my considerable surprise he stopped me saying, 'No, that's just as I want it. I look forward so much to hearing you sing at the Festival.' That was it! It was the only time I ever sang *The Bells* but it will never be forgotten.

That performance introduced me to the glories of Rachmaninov's vocal music and aroused my curiosity, I consequently investigated some of his many songs and took several of them into my repertoire, including *Spring waters, Lilacs, Before my window* and *Christ is risen.*

I worked with Walford Davies on several occasions though never on one of his own compositions. The most memorable was undoubtedly the Royal Command Performance of 1938 which was devised by Sir Walford in his capacity as Master of the King's Musick and which was given on 24 May, Empire Day. This was one of a whole series of notable royal concerts inspired by the outstanding success of George V's silver jubilee concert in 1935. Like its predecessors, the concert was devoted to British music and given at the Royal Albert Hall in the presence of Their Majesties. I started off by singing the song *Down by the crystal spring* unaccompanied in front of the assembled Royal Family and a packed hall including a vast contingent of choirs from every corner of the country. It was, I unhesitatingly admit, one of the most daunting moments of my life. I trembled with nerves though fortunately it did not show in my voice. I remembered my philosophy: concentration upon the job in hand is the only way to conquer nerves. It was an unusual and novel way to start the proceedings and I think it worked. Some of the concert was recorded live by HMV, and the recorded items certainly capture a remarkable atmospheric event.

I was also asked by Sir Walford to sing for him at a concert in Wales though I was quickly nonplussed when I discovered that it was to be held in a marquee. Apparently the concert was part of a little local festival and as there was no hall large enough to house the events the organisers opted for a specially erected tent. I feared singing under canvas and Sir Walford attempted to allay my fears with a healthy shot of flattery – 'With your voice you have no need to bother.' In the final analysis I have to confess I had indeed 'no need to bother' and the concert was a marked success. All the soloists were invited to stay at the Davies's large house which included a magnificent winding staircase in a commanding main hall. At the base of the staircase, Lady Davies had arranged a spectacular floral display in one of the largest bowls I think I have ever seen. Spirits were naturally high after the concert, particularly where my youthful tenor colleague Frank Titterton was concerned. As we were all gathered in the hall prior to retiring Frank eyed this large bowl with sheer devilment and addressed the assembled company. 'Well ladies, it's my bath night tonight, goodnight!' and stepped straight into the bowl. It was typical of him.

I have written earlier at some length about my work with Sir Hamilton Harty; as he was undoubtedly the composer with whom I worked with more than any other in my career he merits further mention here. He had a remarkable sincere modesty about his own compositions. Once when we were about to rehearse his *Ode to a nightingale* at Bradford, to his dismay he discovered that he had forgotten his score. I automatically offered him mine, as I had committed the work to memory and had brought the score along only in case it was necessary to refer to it during rehearsals. He was genuinely touched to discover that I could perform *his* work from memory. From my point of view it was nothing exceptional; I always attempted to memorise the works I sang as I felt that one cannot really interpret unless the work has been totally digested.

Singing without a score of course does have its dangers. Once, singing the *Ode to a nightingale*, I made a slight slip. I felt desolate and apologised profusely to Sir Hamilton. He dismissed it with a kind, benevolent smile and a comforting word or two. He must have realised that my error weighed heavily upon me, however, as he sent the following letter. It is also highly revealing about the extent to which he was prepared to go in order to assist in the improvement of someone he believed in.

28th January, 1927

Dear Bella,

Your singing last night was beautiful, and don't worry over the little slip – that might occur to anyone. There is no doubt in my mind that if you keep your voice as it is at present, and go on improving in style, you will become the leading oratorio and concert English soprano.

I am prepared to help you in any way and so when you need advice or a lesson in style and interpretation, ask me without constraint. I believe I can assist you in such ways. All this is private. I would not do it for anyone but someone, like you, of exceptional talent. You were a good girl last night – go on the same path!

Yours sincerely,
H.H.

In 1936 I was asked by Sir Hamilton to participate with him in a BBC recital devoted exclusively to his songs. It proved so successful that we were asked to sing a second recital – of entirely fresh material. That was highly demanding for his songs were very difficult to interpret properly and he was always most meticulous in what he wanted. The feeling had to be perfectly judged and every point of the score scrupulously observed. He went to endless trouble to teach me these songs. I, of course, was delighted to be on the receiving end, benefiting from his insight. It was after the first of these recitals that he wrote, firstly offering his thanks but then still beavering away at my improvement:

22nd June, 1936

Dear Isobel,

I ought to have written to you a long time ago to say thanks for your singing of my songs, and for all the trouble you took over them. You are a dear. You know that in our work there is no standing still and I think we could still further improve one thing – that is *diction*. The few people whose opinion I respect and trust were unanimous in saying that they thought the *words* could have been clearer. They all recognise what I love above all – the beauty of tone and quality in your singing – but I think it is strength and not weakness to take some notice of obviously friendly and affectionate criticism. Don't you? I believe they are right besides, and while loving and admiring your singing with all my heart, I want to see it perfect in every detail. So will you consider having a few lessons from a past master of diction like H. Plunket Greene?. He's too good an artist to interfere with anything good you do (and that's plenty!) but I believe he could help you immensely in the diction question.

I am proposing the Ode at various places, and hope they come off. That will be great fun.

Best love and good luck,
Yours always
Hay

I obviously dallied somewhat over the question of seeking the advice of Plunket Greene for in less than a fortnight Harty broached the subject again, after first replying to my promise to sing the *Ode* with him in Folkestone.

3rd July, 1936

My dear Isobel,

That's splendid and very good of you. I'll tell them at Folkestone to write to you, being as decent and as generous as they can. It will be very pleasant doing this work again together.

With regard to the 'diction' question, I don't know if you still favour the idea of going to Plunket Greene. I mentioned the possibility to him and he says 'She has one of the purest and loveliest voices I know, and I should be delighted to lend a helping hand there if it is desired'. I hope you don't feel depressed, dear Isobel, that after all this time there should be more work to do on your singing? But that's the way with all of us who take our work seriously — there's *always* more to do if we seek perfection.

You know what ideas I have of you and for you, and so I hope you will stick to the hard and strong path!

Love from
Hay

I have to confess that I never did see Harry Plunket Greene concerning 'the diction question' though this was not because I did not want to improve my diction. Far from it, for that was something I worked on throughout my career. No, sadly Plunket Greene died just over a month later and so I was deprived of this golden opportunity.

As with Eric Fogg's songs, so did Hay's miniature masterpieces stay in my repertoire all my singing life. Some were eventually to be sung in fond remembrance at, for example, a chamber concert held in his memory at the Holst Room at Morley College in 1952 and, more evocative still, at a 1974 recital of music in the parish church at his birthplace, Hillsborough.

CHAPTER EIGHT

Messiah

FOR all the many twentieth-century compositions mentioned in
the last chapter most people who have heard me sing, whether in
the flesh or from broadcasts and recordings, inevitably link my
name to a single composition, one first performed at Dublin in
April 1742 – Handel's *Messiah*. It was a work I sang for over fifty
years yet it always remained a discovery, revealing new depths
and fresh subleties in each performance. I am repeatedly questioned about my approach to *Messiah* and of the memorable experiences which have occurred during a lifetime's acquaintance
with this masterpiece. I consequently seek the reader's permission
to keep chronology at bay for this and the next two chapters
while I deal specifically with *Messiah* and generally about various
vocal matters.

Unbelievable as it might now appear I sang my first *Messiah* at
the age of fifteen in the very city which has for so much of my
life proved my working base, Manchester. I was invited by one
of the local Stretford churches, now sadly demolished, to sing the
soprano solos in a performance accompanied by the church organist. I was a little scared, particularly in *Rejoice greatly*, as I was
then not as confident about those runs as I later became, and, of
course, in *I know that my Redeemer liveth* which always remained
a great challenge. Manchester was, coincidentally, also the loca-
tion of a never-to-be-forgotten performance of *Messiah*, a performance which left a deep impression on me. It was not given
under any particularly grand or momentous circumstance yet it
proved for some inexplicable reason an especially inspired one. It
took place one afternoon in the Zion Hall with the sun shining

97

through the windows at the rear of this great hall. I well remember thinking afterward that that was the standard I wished to emulate in all future *Messiah* performances. Perhaps being 'a believer' helped. I had gone to Sunday School throughout my childhood and had had the sweetest teacher, though I have to confess to being a perfect monkey and giving her a lot of trouble. I don't know why, as I was always so well behaved at my day school! My mother had also sought considerable comfort and solace from religion after the death of my father. Of course, those were the days when one followed one's faith.

Manchester was also the setting for my first 'big' *Messiah*. Hamilton Harty gave me my first *Messiah* with the Hallé Orchestra on a Good Friday in the early 1920s, the very first *Messiah* ever to be broadcast. It was an opportunity I very nearly missed as I was then under contract to William Boosey who, as Robert Elkin rightly states in his book *Queen's Hall 1893–1941*, 'had a dislike of broadcasting amounting almost to a phobia'. In Boosey's eyes artists who broadcast would, in a very short time, lose their live audiences. I was consequently forced to write to Mr Boosey and apply for special permission to broadcast. Much to my surprise dispensation was granted and it was with considerable relief that I joined my 'regular' *Messiah* colleagues, Muriel Brunskill, Heddle Nash and Norman Allin. The performance, which was broadcast throughout Europe, prompted one of the most touching tributes I ever received. It came from a listener in Holland who addressed the postcard to 'The nightingale who sang late in the evening c/o the Hallé Orchestra.' It was delivered to Hamilton Harty who kindly passed it to me remarking, 'This *must* be for you!'

I sang the 'Hallé *Messiah*' for about twenty-six consecutive years. Undeterred by the bombing of the Free Trade Hall during the Second World War, the series continued at Manchester's Belle Vue. It was, in fact, during a Belle Vue performance of *Messiah* that I informed Sir Malcolm Sargent, 'That's my last!' His flattering reply – 'What are you talking about, that was beautiful' – did nothing to dissuade me. I felt I had reached the stage where I might do something I would be ashamed of, that I might spoil the impression I had created all those years. That was something I wished to avoid at all costs; I hated the thought of people saying 'Oh, she should have given up years ago!' Consequently I started to worry about the Hallé performances months before they were due to take place. If I harboured doubts it must surely be time to stop. I continued to sing *Messiah* for many years after that decision but never with the Hallé. Those performances were very special.

It is now impossible to count the number of times I have sung *Messiah* though the final tally must surely be in four figures! Of fifty-one appearances with the Royal Choral Society at the Royal Albert Hall thirty-three were in *Messiah*. I can still feel the awe I experienced when I saw the interior of the Royal Albert Hall for the first time prior to my first *Messiah* there, with Sir Thomas Beecham no less! Standing at the back of that vast auditorium I thought to myself '*This* is my Waterloo!' But I was in for a favourable surprise as although I do not have a big voice it appeared to suit the Albert Hall acoustic very well. Nothing was lost, a fact supported by the story of an Albert Hall habitué telling the person next to him, unbeknown to him a friend of mine, 'This is what we have been waiting for!' The majority of singers dislike performing there but for me it was perfect.

A few days before that first Albert Hall *Messiah* with Beecham I had heard him broadcast the work on my little cat's whisker wireless and was highly alarmed to discover him taking *Rejoice greatly* at almost twice the pace to that which I was accustomed. During rehearsal I was almost trembling in my shoes as *Rejoice* drew inexorably closer but Sir Thomas must have been in an especially mellow mood for as we came to that fateful aria he turned to me, stroked his beard and decreed, 'Take it at your own time, Miss Baillie' which is exactly what Miss Baillie did! I also underwent a similar kind of experience at a later Beecham *Messiah*, this time at Covent Garden (he used to perform *Messiah* there annually with the Covent Garden Chorus and Orchestra). On arriving for the rehearsal I was informed by the friendly baritone that there was to be a cut in *I know that my Redeemer Liveth*. I was dumbfounded. 'A cut in *I know*? Why?' 'Well', came the reply, 'the soprano who sang it last year didn't particularly like the two or three bars with the top G and so they were cut.' Once again I was in fear and trembling though I certainly had no intention of cutting the 'offending bars' for anyone, not even Sir Thomas. When we arrived at the start of the third part I dared to enquire, 'Sir Thomas, do you mind if we reinstate those few bars in *I know that my Redeemer liveth*?' He looked surprised but replied, 'Not at all Miss Baillie'. Then, turning to the orchestra he proclaimed in an especially loud voice, 'Gentlemen, put the bars back in – she wants to sing it *all*!'

My respect for the score was based on the version which was, of course, prevalent during the first decades of this century, the type still to be found in so many homes to this day. Only once, towards the end of my singing career when it became fashionable to add ornamentation to the vocal line, did I sing an 'authentic *Messiah*'. This was for John Tobin who provided added ornamentation for the da capo repeats and, in *Rejoice greatly O daughter of Zion*, some vocalisation after the completion of the aria. I did not approve though, of course, I sang it for Mr Tobin who was conducting the performance. I did not feel that this was Handel and I feel even more strongly about it with each passing year. I have always regarded *Messiah* not as a concert but more as a service and I feel that ornamentation detracts both from the flow of the music and the meaning of the text. When I made my feelings apparent in the BBC television programme *Face the Music* I received many letters supporting this now minority viewpoint. One of the pithiest came from Bernard Shore:

> How deeply refreshing to hear you to-night. Your marvellous punch from the shoulder on all this 'Back to Bach & Handel' nonsense, to hear you singing the actual music without all these idiotic musicological pundits' ornamentations was quite lovely. This so called craze for baroque authenticity has now ruined all our magnificent organs and I am scared to play a Handel Sonata on my instrument for fear of being pilloried because I prefer Handel without frills! What a state we are all in.

I have sung *Messiah* in practically every corner of the British Isles, from London, Belfast, Cardiff and Glasgow to Truro, Carlisle and Aberdeen. Every time I hope I gave a new performance, not always easy at times with such a familiar work. I cannot analyse exactly how I did it but it could have something to do with the fact that I would tell myself that someone in the audience was hearing *Messiah* for the very first time.

Messiah performances were then almost an annual ritual in practically any church which could boast a choir, not only in this country but all over the world where the English language was sung or spoken. It is still a forgone conclusion that a singer will be asked at some stage in her or his career to sing at least one aria for *Messiah*. Because of its familiarity some singers are apt to approach the work too superficially, which is risky because, apart from the fact that most audiences will know practically every note and word of the score, the solos demand an exacting standard from any singer. All facets of the singer's technique are brought into play: phrasing, breath control, agility, diction and, above all, an ability to express and convey the biblical message. The vocal discipline required for *Messiah* will most certainly stand a singer in very good stead for almost any other work.

It is essential that the soloist has complete confidence in his reading, a confidence which stems from long and detailed study. Once every dot of the score has been assimilated the singer can then interpret. I have to admit to not being consciously aware of 'interpreting' as such: it is something which comes almost instinctively because one knows the score so well. Only if there is a complete understanding of the message and picture contained in the text and the notes will your performance linger in the minds of your audience and you will be acclaimed a *real singer* and not merely a vocalist.

In the relatively static world of oratorio, deportment is of major importance. Deportment is not simply the manner in which a singer walks onto the concert platform and conducts himself during the course of his performance. Deportment also includes those long stretches in which you are *not* performing, as well as encompassing your attitude to your fellow artists, not least the conductor who may or may not be of international repute but who is nevertheless in charge of the performance and consequently entitled to your respect. It may be that you feel you know more about the work than he does but it is not really polite to make this evident by your behaviour. You are there solely as a performer and not to play the role of critic. Leave that to the critics! As many performances are given in churches it also behoves the four soloists to dress in a sober fashion. For the ladies I always favoured black or white, or both. One should look attractive but after the initial impression appearances must be forgotten and attention given to the music.

Having sung *Messiah* for more than fifty years my approach to this ever-popular score might be of interest to singers and would-be singers alike. I therefore conclude this chapter with a brief examination of the key recitatives and arias. However, before doing so it would, perhaps, be beneficial to consider the very different qualities of the three sections which comprise *Messiah:*

Part 1, the narration of the Christmas story, is by its very nature open, simple and joyous. Part 2 graphically depicts Christ's anguish and suffering, and contains strong and vivid emotions; the general tenor of Part 3 falls somewhere between these two extremes and is concerned primarily with consolation, comfort and ultimately salvation.

First, the tenor recitative *Comfort ye* and aria *Ev'ry valley shall be exalted*. The elevated note of the first syllable of 'comfort' is easier to pitch if you enunciate the first consonant rather strongly. This will place the tone in the correct position. The recitative itself should be sung with the ever-present thought that people everywhere need comfort. The tone employed should consequently be as warm as possible. This recitative should also not be too loud, the accompaniment will not intrude. The final section of the recitative, 'The voice of him that crieth in the wilderness', is another matter. It should be sung with solid tone and in real recitative-like, declamatory manner, with the conviction of a true prophet. The aria should contain good phrasing and an easy vocal tone. Respect the *Andante* marking for it should not be too quick.

The prophetic attitude should also be well in evidence in the bass recitative *Thus saith the Lord, the Lord of hosts* and aria *But who may abide the day of His coming*. Great dignity and full vocal tone are required as well as a decisive attitude: this is truth and there must be no room for doubt. When 'And who shall stand when He appeareth?' is reached it should be sung a little more softly, even with a sense of doubt as to *who* actually will be participating in the glorious coming of Christ. Great contrast can be employed when singing 'For he is like a refiner's fire'. Here is positive truth again, nothing is doubtful, and all should be expressed via solid singing and clarity of text.

Contrary to a great many performances the contralto recitative and aria *Behold! A virgin shall conceive* and *O thou that tellest good tidings to Zion* are an expression of great joy and should therefore be sung with confident, real tone. The words can be used to attain this end. The recitative needs a rather gentle treatment at the phrase 'and bear a son' though happiness should still predominate. The aria itself should be rhythmic from beginning to end and there should be no unsettling *rallentando* before the chorus enter.

The recitative *For behold, darkness shall cover the earth* and the aria *The people that have walked in darkness have seen a great light* present the bass with a real opportunity to display his command of vocal colour. The recitative is highly atmospheric and should convey a certain terror at the thought of abysmal darkness. When 'But the Lord shall arise upon thee' is reached the great relief which would be experienced in the coming of the Lord must be evident both in the singer's approach and from his tonal colour. A similar approach is required in the aria. Not too slow a tempo should be adopted, it is after all marked *larghetto*.

All this considerable time the soprano has been seated waiting for her first entry. It is essential that she should do nothing to attract attention to herself. I have sometimes been appalled by the disrespect some singers have shown both for their conductors and for the work they are singing. I remember on one occasion during a performance of *Messiah* in Blackpool when the soprano decided not to go onto the platform with her colleagues at the start of the performance: she made an entrance when it was her turn to sing! The performance continued uninterrupted until the baritone completed his final solo, *The trumpet shall sound*. He then took his revenge by demonstratively walking off stage! The soprano should stand during the rising phrase in the penultimate bar of the Pastoral Symphony, keeping perfectly still (unnoticed if possible) until the opening chord of the recitative *There were shepherds abiding in the fields*. Imagination can then be employed! I always envisaged a dark blue, star-studded sky, the lonely shepherds and the feel of the chill night air. Make a dramatic pause before the voice enters with 'There were shepherds' and keep the reiterated quavers calm and steady by lengthening the quaver rests! A quiet *larghetto* can then be achieved. 'And lo!' should be about *mezzo forte*, full tone should not be used until 'the glory of the Lord', is reached and a *diminuendo* can be employed in 'sore afraid'. The second recitative, *And the angel said unto them* is *parlando* and should give the impression of coming nearer to your audience as if to tell a story. If being phrased as speech some of the rests can be eliminated. A warmer tone and a little *tenuto* should be used at 'a Saviour' and the last phrase, 'which is Christ the Lord', should be in one breath and *fortissimo*. Excitement is the key-word in the third recitative, *And suddenly there was with the angel*, the first phrase concluding only at 'of the heav'nly host'. The last phrase, 'praising God and saying' requires no *ritardando*; full, glorious tone will suffice. Do not hold onto the top A of 'saying' as a steady tempo is required for the *attacca* chorus *Glory of God*. These three recitatives demand a tremendous range both vocally and emotionally, so much so that it might be necessary to remind oneself of the dividing line between opera and oratorio; I always consider it bad taste to use 'gulps' and such like to convey emotion.

The excitement of the recitative *And suddenly* should be carried over into the aria *Rejoice greatly*, which is not a vehicle for technical display, though the runs, of course, must be clear and each taken in a single breath. Begin the two longest runs rather more softly and hold the breath back, using the absolute minimum for sustaining vocal tone. Then, when about halfway through and secure in the knowledge that you can safely 'stay the course', you can conclude the run with a crescendo. Sing the repeated 'rejoice' first softly and then with full voice, forming the word with strong consonants and keeping the tone in position. Use the word 'greatly' both to illustrate and to provide relief after the rigid control required by the runs. The central section of the aria, *He is the righteous Saviour*, should always begin at the same tempo; it will get slower of its own accord. The final phrase, 'He shall speak peace unto the heathen', should be a soft *pianissimo* to heighten the contrast with the return of *Rejoice greatly*. The singer must now re-establish and maintain at 'white heat' that sense of excitement. Very little *ritardando* is required at the end, simply a sense of joy.

The contralto should convey a sense of miracle in the recitative *Then shall the eyes*; the aria *He shall feed his flock* should then be sung with a flowing *legato* to express His regard and concern. I used to employ a pleading approach with the soprano entrance *Come unto Him all ye that Labour*, rather like a minister in a pulpit, which gives a different colour and quality. I remember with gratitude a young curate coming to me after a performance of *Messiah* saying 'I know exactly what you were conveying in *Come unto Him* and I felt you were singing it just for me.' A simple compliment but one to treasure.

For all the stark emotions to be found in Part 2 there is nevertheless an underlying thread of consolation which underpins the entire section and must never be lost from sight. Such complexities mean that the solos have to be especially well studied and given very considerable thought. In the contralto aria *He was despised and rejected* the singer must convey a heartfelt sincerity and produce the darkest tone quality possible. Many might not be aware that this popular piece is in fact a da capo aria with a contrasting central section, *He gave his back to the smiters.* This makes the aria particularly long, but with careful and imaginative handling momentum can be maintained and the overall structure sustained. Certainly for musical balance the inclusion of the central section is essential. There follows an unusual succession of four choruses after which the Passion music commences. This consists of the recitatives and arias *Thy rebuke hath broken His heart* and *Behold, and see if there be any sorrow,* followed by *He was cut off out of the land of the living* and *But Thou didst not leave His soul in Hell.* The crucial responsibility for the entire narration of this dark tragedy falls entirely upon the tenor who must sing with great stillness and sorrow, the voice alone conveying the exceptional sadness of this episode. The omission of the tenor recitative *Unto which the angels* together with the chorus *Let all the angels of God worship him* is common. The music here is less inspired and its omission reduces the work's overall duration while in no way detracting from the story.

The bass solo *Thou art gone up on high* must be sung with a firm vocal tone. This is a joyous aria and must not sound grim and determined no matter how difficult the vocal line appears. The soprano aria *How beautiful are the feet* should be sung with radiant purity. To me this is a direct message to priests and ministers, conveying the importance of their duties. The bass aria *Why do the nations?* requires exceptionally fine singing; flexible, even runs which should not be sung in an empty, coloratura manner but one which must convey an imposing strength and conviction. This can be best achieved by not rushing the pace. I would commend the cautionary qualification *poco* to Handel's *Allegro* marking. The tenor must not hesitate to 'point' the crucial words 'scorn' and 'derision' in his recitative *He that dwelleth in heaven shall laugh them to scorn.* The ensuing aria *Thou shalt break them* is by no means easy to sing but will be made easier if the *Andante* marking is observed.

Part 3 opens with the quietude of the soprano aria *I know that my Redeemer liveth,* a dramatic contrast to the fiery magnificence of the *Hallelujah Chorus* which brought Part 2 to such a triumphant conclusion. This aria does not exist as a display piece and must convey a sense of quiet conviction and assurance. Once again, imagination plays a great part in the rendition of this aria; in my mind I always picture myself standing by His graveside. The opening section *I know that my Redeemer liveth* in particular demands a feeling of total conviction yet must be sung quite naturally. I recommend some minor adjustments to the distribution of the words in the second lengthy vocal phrase so that the music and text flow more naturally – even in the most up-to-date and ruthlessly 'authentic' versions amendments to Handel's phrasing of 'and that he shall stand at the latter day upon the earth' are made:

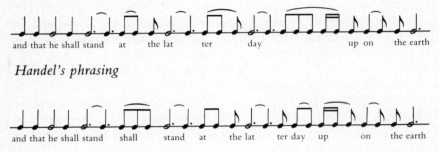

Handel's phrasing

My recommended phrasing

I learnt this phrasing from Madam Sadler-Fogg who I suspect inherited it from Marchesi. It is of considerable assistance if the orchestra can be persuaded into making a *pianissimo diminuendo* in the two bars which precede the terrifying thought of 'and tho' worms destroy this body' which should be sung as quietly as possible: it is marked only *piano* but I would always try to achieve a *pianissimo* here. Joy should enter the voice on reaching the phrase 'Yet in my flesh I shall see God', dispelling the horror of the previous phrase. During the closing lines of this aria I would also recommend a pause on the top G of the word 'risen' in the second repeat of the phrase 'For now is Christ risen', emphasising that positive triumph is uppermost. Let this held note die away gradually so that the phrase remains sustained. The final phrase 'the first fruits of them that sleep' should be sung as softly as possible, as if in the presence of those who *are* asleep. Do not hesitate to extend the 's' of 'sleep' so that it is audible. Harty alone continued the *pianissimo* hush of this aria by reducing the accompaniment to a string quartet in the orchestral postlude; a marvellous, magical conclusion. Though unorthodox it was an approach which pre-echoed the ensuing vocal quartets *Since by man came death* and *For as in Adam all die*, the only occasion the four soloists are required to sing together as a team. The voices may at times prove somewhat disparate but it will hardly be noticeable if Handel's *pianissimo* marking is observed.

The bass recitative *Behold, I tell you a mystery* should begin in a subdued manner, almost muffled, though gaining focus as the recitative progresses so that all is clarion-like clarity by the concluding phrase 'at the last trumpet'. In the aria *The trumpet shall sound* respect both the *pomposo* marking as well as Handel's *ma non* qualification to the *Allegro*. This aria requires very careful observance of dynamics and abundant vocal tone. The contralto recitative *Then shall be brought to pass* and the tenor-contralto duet *O death where is thy sting* are rarely sung. Both pieces prove an anticlimax to *The trumpet shall sound* and prevent the latter's heady propulsion into the chorus *But thanks be to God*. Likewise, the soprano aria *If God be with us, who can be against us* is also frequently omitted. If included it provides the soprano with a welcome contrast to the tension of *I know that my Redeemer liveth* and must be sung with the greatest joy and fullest vocal tone possible. At all times the crucial dynamic markings and expressive text must be observed. The runs on the word 'intercession' are impossible to execute accurately and with a pleasing tone unless the 'e' vowel sound is adapted to an 'ae' sound, placed in the mouth where the 'a' vowel is produced. It must be a very positive solo which leads to the work's triumphant climax in the choruses *Worthy is the lamb* and *Amen*.

CHAPTER NINE

Vocal Matters

Now is probably an appropriate time to 'talk turkey' concerning vocal matters. Everyone with any interest in singers and singing is fascinated by the capabilities of the human voice – how it is able to produce sounds of such variety and contrast. Differences in sound between the great instrumentalists, even when citing such pianistic opposites as Richter and Rubinstein, are largely obvious only to a discriminating ear, yet the differences in sound between the great vocalists, for example de los Angeles, Callas, Schwarzkopf and Sutherland to name four prima donnas active during my day, are instantly recognisable. Startlingly different sounds are produced from the same instrument, the human throat.

I have always been a natural lyric soprano. I do not think my voice has basically changed even from my teenage years. I made no attempt to extend my vocal range either up or down, first because I was quite content with the voice I was fortunate enough to possess, and secondly for fear of emitting a noise which would have sounded false and unnatural. I was always confident and happy as far as top B, and top C also came readily within my range. Only if there were several in succession, for example in such a work as Kodály's *Missa brevis*, where the soprano line contains a liberal sprinkling of top Cs, did they become noticeable.

I have always maintained that the more natural the voice the more beautiful it will be. When a student first comes to me I always try to ascertain how naturally he or she sings and subsequently attempt to build upon that. I can, for instance, point out certain aspects which might improve what is already being done though I always try to refrain from assuming a dictatorial stance with an inflexible list of 'do's' and 'don'ts'. Each pupil is an individual with different requirements and difficulties. What I do try to maintain at all costs is the natural foundation upon which to build.

I have never been aware of vibrato, and have never consciously attempted to add vibrato to my singing. Vibrato came simply with the emotion I was feeling, just as did my tonal colour. Of course, I came from an era when vibrato was rather frowned upon. Nowadays the vibrato one constantly hears is, to my mind, bad singing: a vaguely pitched, wide-wobbling noise involving at least *two* notes rather than natural vocal movement centred upon a single note. While I do not wish to give the impression that I am anti-stage I do lay the blame for this at the feet of opera. Singers are inclined to go into opera far too young, long before they know their vocal capabilities. I in no way wish to set myself up as an example but personally I did not venture into opera until I was forty-five, by which time I certainly knew my capabilities! On stage singers are constantly asked to do things which they are not required to do on the concert platform and it is these extra demands which frequently prove excessive and force a young singer into pushing his or her voice unnaturally. This is when an innate vibrato will start to collapse into an intrusive beat.

It is impossible to recommend a single vocal method. Indeed I would go as far as to state that when a method is *imposed* upon a singer the voice will undoubtedly lose its spontaneity and freshness as well as its natural tone and character. In short, a natural voice should require no set method. The use of method can, of course, be of assistance in helping singers who are experiencing vocal difficulties. 'Method' must not be equated with exercises. All voices have to be exercised though never to the extent of hour after hour every day; this is not only quite unnecessary but can also prove harmful. One does not need to exercise scales, vowels and consonants for more than half-an-hour a day at the very most.

My earliest lessons with Madam Sadler-Fogg concentrated a great deal upon breathing exercises and it consequently became second nature to me to breathe in the right way. All my life I have used the method devised by the famous nineteenth-century-born singing teacher, William Shakespeare, himself a pupil of the legendary Lamperti. It is a method which has always stood me in great stead. If ever I encountered any worries or problems I would simply return to my breathing. When that is correct all else is almost certain to fall into place. There are naturally many component parts concerned with the intricacies of singing but correct breathing is, I think, of paramount importance.

The Shakespeare method is one that never lets a singer down. It involves the intake and exhalation of air by the muscular control of the diaphragm. The breath must always be taken through the mouth rather than the nose – nasal breathing is both obvious and audible and is thus far too distracting to the audience – and has to be positioned in the diaphragm. This can be achieved only by abdominal breathing which enables additional space for air around the back below the rib cage. Shoulders must remain still and never raised and the chest kept erect. The arms should hang freely and naturally, not clenched by the side of the body, with the hands held gently in front of the diaphragm. I also used to begin singing with my lips slightly parted. Consequently many people would comment that they never saw me take a breath. With the mouth open already to sing and the hands in front of the diaphragm it is an illusion which is by no means difficult to achieve. The only tension in the body should be the diaphragm; the jaw in particular should remain flexible at all times.

The actual vocal sound is, of course, created by the emission of this breath. This act of emission is achieved by the muscular control of the diaphragm. The louder one sings the more breath is needed. The quieter one sings the greater muscular control is required in order to maintain vocal support. The throat will respond accordingly. I think it is quite unnecessary for the throat to be held in a certain fixed position or that the palate must be moulded in a particular manner. The natural response of the throat and mouth to secure, firm breathing can be taken for granted.

The mouth is necessary for the projection and the quality of the sound being created and should consequently never be slack. The numerous little muscles surrounding the lips are responsible for the projection of vocal tone. It is not simply a matter of opening one's mouth and emitting a noise, it has to be directed, rather like making a funnel. The quality of the vocal tone is largely dictated by the vowel sounds which, in turn, are controlled by the shape of the mouth. When the mouth is rounded the tone is consequently 'covered' and beautiful. The opposite is the hard, ugly tone of a mouth with 'corners'. A rounded mouth might occasionally involve an adjusted vowel sound – 'tander' rather than 'tender', for example – especially on higher notes. These are the final adjustments left to the singer.

I have been fortunate in experiencing few vocal problems during my career. I attribute this largely to the superb groundwork of my early years, plus the fact that I never taxed my voice. Such few problems that I did encounter were more mental than physical, a common occurrence with singers. Sometimes I might sing a work too often and would, as a result, become over-anxious concerning a certain phrase which would suddenly appear 'difficult'. One such example was the opening phrase of Handel's *Art thou troubled?* which for no apparent reason suddenly began to worry me unduly. I consequently put the aria out of sight for several weeks, if not a little more, and when I eventually returned to it the 'problem' had disappeared. It was simply a case of over-familiarity. Once I also developed the problem of over-salivating. Many might react by instantly rushing to their doctor or their nearest vocal teacher. I simply 'sweated it out' and the problem went away of its own accord. When one experiences a psychological problem the only thing to do if possible is to leave it well alone for a while.

Should there be something wrong with the voice then action must, of course, be taken. This is when a method can be employed. Sometimes the wrong vowels are used or the consonants are too weak to place the tone in the correct position. (How useful, for example, is the trick of using a preceding consonant as a launching pad to place an open vowel sound of a following high note.) The majority of vocal problems, however, appear to stem from over-taxing the voice resulting in a lack of basic control. I have had pupils come to see me with an intrusive beat which has appeared quite uncontrollable. One way to attempt regaining control is to make the unfortunate sufferer sing sitting down; the voice cannot be 'pushed' from such a position.

I have also had pupils with problems concerning the way they behave on the concert platform. One girl, for example, was unable to stand and sing a song without adding a physical running commentary with her entire body. I consequently gave her Vaughan Williams's *Silent noon* to sing, a song of great tranquillity but great intensity, and made her stand perfectly still. The realisation that it was possible to sing without excessive movement

111

began to dawn. 'But it's so much easier!' she exclaimed in total astonishment. This is not to claim that singing must be inanimate, but the face is quite capable of mirroring all the emotions of the text. And so much can be done with the eyes!

I have encountered some singers so obsessed by the mechanics of singing that they have become totally rigid. The only recourse is to get them to unwind. The throat can be freed to some extent by placing the tongue on the lower teeth: the throat opens naturally, enabling the sound to flow freely again. This is why I firmly believe that singing must be a totally natural process and that the less aware one is of the mechanics so much the better. Let the pupil sing and see what needs to be done – if anything!

Singing must always be a joy and never a trouble.

Summing up, I think the following six hints will contribute towards a successful and happy singing career:

1. Singing is a natural process and the more naturally the sound is made the more beautiful a sound will emerge.
2. Handel and Mozart for discipline!
3. Be a singer expressing emotions, not merely a vocalist. Audiences know the difference and so will you by their reaction!
4. Choose repertoire which suits your voice and personality.
5. Keep within your vocal and interpretative limits.
6. Always *listen* to the sound you make and *never sing louder than lovely*.

CHAPTER TEN

In Front of the Microphone

DURING a long career visits to studios, be they for broadcasting or recording, become part of a way of life. However, few musicians, I think, ever feel entirely at ease in such surroundings, particularly if the only audience is the cold, impersonal microphone. But a deep breath is drawn, a brave face assumed and an adventure begun. Today the very mention of the word studio conjures up for most people a recording studio where I was, indeed, a frequent vistor during a period of fifty years. But there are also imperishable memories of the broadcasting studio, both radio and television.

Broadcasting was very much in its infancy during the initial years of my singing professionally in the early 1920s: we collided more or less head on. I made my very first broadcast from Trafford Park in Manchester in the days before there was even a BBC. It proved an amazing experience. The broadcast took the form of a popular ballad concert with husband Harry contributing the 'comic songs' and myself the other vocal items. Jo Lamb provided some violin solos and the versatile accompanist and occasional piano soloist was John Wills. The surviving photograph still raises a smile. The primitive broadcasting studio looks incapable of transmitting sound more than a few yards, while I look more like my grandmother than a girl in her mid-twenties, a graphic reminder of how my weight has always tended to fluctuate, fortunately, though, never to the detriment of my voice. I would, for example, certainly not side with those singers who maintain that to lose weight also means losing one's voice; when I first started to sing I was a mere eight-stone slip of a girl and did not gain weight until I became a mother in 1918. When I later lost weight it made not a scrap of difference to my voice. This is not to say, of course, that a singer must have a certain 'bulk', but an excess of weight is simply a nuisance.

How rapidly broadcasting techniques advanced and how extraordinary that, coincidentally, I always appeared to be on hand as each breakthough occurred. It was not long after that début broadcast that, still in Manchester, I participated in the first ever broadcast of a complete *Messiah* (which I have already mentioned in Chapter 8), and my first visits to London coincided with the flourishing early years of national broadcasting by the BBC. Within a comparatively short while the BBC had become part and parcel of the British way of life, and I was broadcasting regularly from the capital. All seemed set and cosy when the outbreak of the Second World War taught us all to take a quick but hard look at what we were doing and to diversify. Soon the range of broadcasts in which one participated was such that a recital of twentieth-century English songs would be followed the next day by such wartime heroics as *Workers' Playtime* or perhaps a popular type of programme such as Doris Arnold's *These you have loved*. It meant that a Saturday could be spent working with that great Liverpudlian comedian Tommy Handley in Bury while the Sunday would find me in Bristol collaborating with Count John McCormack.

How well I remember a *These you have loved* programme broadcast from Bristol with McCormack and Gerald Moore. When we returned to the hotel after the broadcast the general consensus appeared to be that the programme had gone smoothly and successfully. Inevitably generalisations gave way to specifics and the producer made reference to my singing of Mendelssohn's *On wings of song*. McCormack could not resist an interjection: 'Ah, very nice', he purred, 'but it was too slow, Isobel.' Galant Gerald, ready as ever to defend the underdog, instantly riposted, 'Oh, come now John, it's all right at that speed if you have the breath!' John fell silent and I was vindicated.

I also undertook a great deal of broadcasting, especially for the Continent. The venue for such programmes varied considerably, but the grandest was for a wartime broadcast which came from an aristocratic home 'somewhere in the middle of England' and which, when I arrived, transpired to be near Evesham in Worcestershire. Every tap in the house was gold, while in the garden

114

of the nearby country hotel, luxurious and isolated, was the most beautiful mulberry tree, laden with the largest and tastiest fruit I have ever encountered, in addition to a magnificent Crusader Oak. Just for that day the war seemed a lifetime away.

It might come as something of a surprise that I was also in at the very infancy of British television which, during the prewar years, went out live from Alexandra Palace. Initial experiments in transmitting opera on television began in 1936, though my involvement did not occur until early in 1938 when it was decided to tackle the complete second act of *Tristan and Isolde* with Walter Widdop and myself in the title roles. Walter was a popular and highly successful Tristan though I was no Isolde! It was Hyam Greenbaum, then Television Music Director, who insisted, much to the BBC's general consternation, that I sing Isolde as he firmly maintained that the role demanded a lyric rather than a dramatic soprano. 'Bumps', as he was for some inexplicable reason always known, was a quite remarkable musical all-rounder: not only had he been principal second violin of the Queen's Hall Orchestra and pianist to the Diaghilev Ballet but he had also been a member of the Brosa Quartet and Musical Director of the Cochran reviews!

I realised that I was far from being a natural Isolde but I did enjoy every minute of the adventure. For the transmission the singers were placed off-screen in one studio while actors mimed the actions (but not the words) in front of cameras in another studio. Two performances (afternoon and evening) were given on 24 January 1938 with the event being somewhat mysteriously billed as 'a masque to the music of Wagner'. Walter's and my visual counterparts were Oriel Ross and Basil Bartlett; the other singers were Gwladys Garside (Brangäne), Robert Easton (King Mark) and George Baker (Kurwenal and Melot).

Weeks later I was back in the same studios for a performance of Handel's *Acis and Galatea*. My Acis was Parry Jones – he was kept busy as he also doubled the part of Damon - and Henry Cummings sang the role of the giant Polyphemus. By now it had been decided to broadcast the performances on two different days, 24 April and 3 May 1938. Without exception we were all carried along on what was undoubtedly the pioneering spirit universal at this time. We were only too aware that these broadcasts were received by a mere handful of privileged viewers – the estimated figure seemed to be a little over twenty thousand within a thirty-mile area of Alexandra Palace - but it in no way detracted

115

from our enjoyment or the stimulation of those early days of television.

It is, however, the less ephemeral world of recording which has seen my greatest preoccupation with studios and the like. I made my first recording shortly after my early broadcasts, but I can only piece together the information from scraps of evidence to hand as I have no recollections of the making of my first record, an acoustic HMV test. But the EMI archives do contain evidence of this and I have a broken disc of *One morning very early* which plainly states a recording date of 19 February 1924. Why nothing came of this preliminary foray into the mysterious world of recording I really do not know. It could be that the acoustic process of recording was then dying out and the discs were put to one side, or that 'those in high places' did not find my voice either suitable or acceptable.

My second encounter with a recording company, the Columbia Graphophone Company, then very much a rival of HMV, could however, never be forgotten. It was Sir Hamilton Harty, then musical adviser to Columbia, who secured an audition for me. I came down to London in February 1926 in order to make a series of tests. Quite naturally I felt somewhat apprehensive though I gained more than a degree of comfort knowing that Sir Hamilton was to be my accompanist. I duly arrive at the prearranged time only to discover to my horror that I had arrived at the wrong studios and that I was due at the Columbia studios in Petty France, the other side of the city! What vestige of composure I had mustered had totally vanished by the time I finally arrived at the correct address but Sir Hamilton, who had been there all morning working with Casals, quickly put me at my ease. We recorded tests of Wakefield Cadman's *At dawning* and Sullivan's *Orpheus and his lute*. They proved successful and within days I commenced recording for the Columbia Graphophone Company.

I made the regrettable error of accepting a flat fee for each title, as did so many recording artists at this time, rather than insisting on a royalty rate. Once again I failed to make my fortune. That such a decision proved to be a mistake is illustrated by a story connected with the only *verismo* opera recording I ever made, the love duet from *Madam Butterfly* with Francis Russell. Many years later I met my gramophone Pinkerton in South Africa and inevitably we began to reminisce. The conversation came around to recordings and we fondly recalled that one and only title we made together in 1929. 'Do you know', he proudly claimed, 'I've made a pretty penny out of that one!' With my flat fee I simply could not compete and so remained mute!

My contract was for one year with a two-year renewal clause though it lasted in effect until October 1932. The sole major undertaking of this period was the first 'complete' recording of Mendelssohn's *Elijah* which was conducted by Stanford Robinson and recorded during February 1930 in the Central Hall, Westminster, with Clara Serena, Parry Jones and Harold Williams. It was released as a series of ten-inch records, a somewhat unusual choice for what was then such an ambitious project and one which would automatically appear to dictate a twelve-inch disc format. The latter would have been a far less cumbersome format for the purchaser but the former undoubtedly proved to be musically advantageous, enabling an aria such as *Hear ye Israel* to be comfortably spread across two ten-inch sides of some six minutes' total duration rather than accommodated onto a single twelve-inch side of less than five minutes. The tempi of this first version are therefore far more characteristic of a concert performance than the later recording on twelve-inch discs.

Once again only the physical existence of the discs tells me that I actually recorded *Elijah* in 1930 for I remember nothing about it. This is very much in contrast to the second recording, also undertaken by Columbia, which was made in 1947 at Huddersfield Town Hall. Sir Malcolm Sargent conducted and I joined Gladys Ripley, James Johnston and, of course, Harold Williams. Poor Harold arrived tired and in the midst of an exceptionally busy period. Further more, in those austere post-war years, the entire recording had to be completed in four consecutive days. It was impossibly demanding on Harold who bore the brunt of the entire oratorio. Needless to say he coped magnificently, and Elijah's character grew in stature as each side was completed. Not that the other soloists have an easy time for they are responsible for the numerous contrasting characters who people this highly dramatic score, so dramatic that I always feel that *Elijah* should be termed an oratorio–opera. The soprano, for example, has to be several kinds of singer in order to encompass the varied roles which come her way: the distraught widow in the wilderness in the great duet *What have I to do with thee?* with Elijah – one of the great dramatic moments in all oratorio – the youth sent to spy

117

for rain clouds, and an unusual cross between a priestess and a kind of angel in *Hear ye Israel*.

That later *Elijah* recording was made during my second period with Columbia which commenced in 1941 after ten years in the wilderness, as it were. My first contract expired, as did so many, when the full force of the recession crippled the country during the 1930s. But with the outbreak of the Second World War many foreign artists became unavailable and so many of us natives were invited back into the recording studios. Such an invitation by no means relieved the personal feelings of chagrin that the very years when I considered myself to be at my peak had, by and large, been neatly avoided by the recording companies! During this second period with Columbia I came in contact with Walter Legge who, during the late 1940s and 50s, was responsible for transforming Columbia into this country's greatest classical label. He was at practically all my sessions and seemed to be in control of every aspect of what was by now a highly complicated exercise. We did not always agree on everything though we did for the most part see eye to eye on the basics. Surprisingly for someone as vocally aware as was Walter, he did not always appreciate all the problems a singer had to face. Once when I arrived at the studios for a session, a popular soprano of her time was still busy recording and so I waited in the control room. I instantly realised that she was experiencing considerable vocal difficulties and so began to admonish Walter. 'You really shouldn't let her sing like that, Walter, the poor girl's suffering from laryngitis.' He wouldn't believe me and thought she was simply experiencing an off day. The poor girl valiantly struggled on.

For me I think the most significant outcome of this second period with Columbia, which was to last for ten years, was the 1946 recording of *Messiah* made with Gladys Ripley, James Johnston and Norman Walker and conducted by Sir Malcolm Sargent again in Huddersfield Town Hall. Like Harold during his second *Elijah* recording, this *Messiah* not only coincided with a particularly busy period for me but also had to be completed in a very short period. All my solos were recorded in a single day. On reflection I think I would have done better if they had been spread over at least a couple of days but such a luxury was impossible in those days. I was totally exhausted after having completed my solos and, perhaps fearing a fainting soprano on his hands, I was taken out to dinner by one of the directors of the Huddersfield

Choral Society. It was much needed and greatly appreciated! If ever I put my heart into anything it was that recording. I felt so strongly that it had to be as good as possible, for if my name was linked with one work above all other it was *Messiah*. It was, and remains a daunting thought that this recording was an ineradicable document. I consequently gave it everything I possessed, right from my boots. How strange that this was the first modern recording of *Messiah* and only the second ever to have been made in this country yet it has never been transferred to LP. The Huddersfield Town Hall was for me the finest hall to sing in and it was consequently very comforting to be working in a building I knew intimately. I can still picture myself now, standing on the stage and singing out into the empty hall as if it were full of people.

During the recording I had a minor contretemps with Lawrance Collingwood who was monitoring the recording from the basement. At one point Collingwood emerged looking very worried: I had sung a phrase different from that printed in the score though in a manner long considered traditional. I let my feelings be known to Sargent. 'What does he mean, that's the way its *always* sung!', I insisted with some annoyance. As ever the diplomatic Sargent poured oil onto troubled waters, sweeping the incident aside with quiet reassurance. The temperature subsided and the recording continued amicably. The traditional phrasing remained!

During my years 'in the wilderness' I was occasionally approached by other companies. One was HMV, by now a member of the EMI family along with its once great rival Columbia. In 1945 I participated in a recording of Purcell's *Dido and Aeneas* directed by Constant Lambert. The title roles were sung by Joan Hammond and Dennis Noble with Edith Coates as a particularly venomous Sorceress and myself as Belinda. Boris Ord, who contributed the harpsichord continuo in the Purcell, later directed a series of Elizabethan madrigal recordings which I shared with Margaret Field-Hyde, Gladys Winmill, René Soames and Keith Falkner. There were also the HMV live recordings of the 1938 Empire Day Royal Command Concert given in the Royal Albert Hall, which I have already mentioned in Chapter 7. Finally for HMV came Sir Thomas Beecham's idea of including me in his projected recording of Handel's *Solomon*. He had in mind one of the mezzo-soprano solos which I felt did not really suit me, unlike the exceptionally beautiful *With thee th' unsheltered moor* which I

had already recorded for Columbia. I dutifully made a test recording in the mid-1950s for Sir Thomas but asked for it to be
scrapped as I felt it was not up to standard. I might have missed
being included in Sir Thomas's *Solomon* recording, now something of a vintage item, but I felt it unwise to participate in a
recording simply for the sake of it.

I had just two excursions into Decca's studios. One in the
mid-1930s was made solely to record a pot-pourri, a 'selection'
as they were popularly called in those days, of the hit numbers
from the 1935 Grace Moore film *On Wings of Song*. This con-
densed 'cover version' of the several hit songs included in the
film, also recorded by Grace Moore, ranged from *Mimi's farewell*
and *Musetta's waltz song* from *La Bohème* to the Quartet from
Rigoletto (the other lines taken by the chorus) via *Funiculi Funicula*
and *Love Me Forever* (the film's American title). In December 1953
I participated, at the composer's behest, along with John Cameron
in the first recording of Vaughan Williams's Sea Symphony conducted by Sir Adrian Boult and recorded in the Kingsway Hall.
Recorded in the presence of the composer it appeared at the time
a splendid manner in which to conclude my adventures in the
recording studio.

Twenty-one years later, however, in August 1974 I did make
a return visit to the famous EMI studios in St John's Wood, where
so many of my Columbia recordings were made during the 1940s
and 50s. This came about from a casual remark made to an EMI
producer that I was still singing at my lectures and talks. So was
born the idea of recording some songs which could form part of
a two-record anthology designed to celebrate my eightieth birthday. Thus I was able to do something I had always wanted, to
pay tribute to Sir Hamilton Harty for his invaluable advice and
encouragement by commercially recording more of his songs.
The final side of the anthology, devoted to British songs, commenced with Cadman's *At dawning*, one of those early test records
made with Hay at the piano in 1926 and not previously published,
and concluded with his *The stranger's grave* and *Grace for light*
recorded forty-eight years later.

My accompanist on this occasion was Ivor Newton who later
confided to the producer that he had decided that this afternoon
of music-making would be his very last professional engagement
and that he 'couldn't think of a better way to go!' Ivor had, I
think, reached his 'octogenarian age' just before me (his age was

always his best kept secret), yet he proved, as always, a remark-ably sympathetic accompanist. I do have to plead guilty to spring-ing the Harty songs upon him without any preparation and they took their inevitable toll. After three hours of hard, intensive labours I had to leave the studios in something of a hurry and so bid Ivor a fond if somewhat hasty farewell. I was later told by the producer that after he had seen me off the premises he returned to the studios to discover Ivor literally slumped across the key-board in a state of utter collapse. 'Ivor', he cautiously enquired, 'can I get you a car or a taxi?' Ivor apparently lifted his head sideways, opened one eye and replied in his inimitable dry drawl, 'I think an *ambulance* might be more appropriate!'

After so many paragraphs concerned with recording the ad-mission that I never did really enjoy the experience might come as something of a surprise. It is, however, a feeling which I later discovered to be very typical of many who enter the recording studio. Much of the misgiving arises from an inner feeling that no matter how good the final approved 'take' is it could still be better. Granting artistic approval to a 'take' requires much courage and a considerable degree of compromise. But perhaps I was most disillusioned with the technical problems I encountered on every visit to the recording studio, even in the technologically advanced 1970s; in fact the more sophisticated the microphones became, the more complex became the problems. There appeared to be a basic incompatibility between my voice and the microphone which affected my recordings in two ways. First, practically all the notes above the stave had to be sung with my head turned away from the microphone, thus robbing the climactic passages of their full effect, graphically evident in the 1953 recording of Vaughan Williams's Sea Symphony and still evident in the stereo recordings of 1974. Secondly, the microphone seemed insensitive to the dynamic shading of my singing, the contrast between *mezzo forte* and *forte* or between *forte* and *fortissimo*, so that many of my recordings appear dynamically monotonous. Perhaps these problems could be technically or electronically analysed, though I feel the root cause is that the purity and clarity of sound which I always strove for are alien to the microphone. I feel that both the public and myself have been robbed.

I do feel, however, favourably inclined towards a few of my recordings, for example that of Purcell's *Blessed Virgin's expostu-lation*. I had a real fight on my hands to persuade Columbia to let me record this title as they felt it would be uncommercial. I had adored the piece since I had heard it sung by Dorothy Silk at a Hallé concert sometime in the 1920s and was determined to record it one day, though it took ten years before I was able to sing it in the manner I felt it deserved. I am pleased to have recorded both *Messiah* and *Elijah* even if the former is not 'authentic' in the manner currently fashionable. As I have already pointed out, I have never really favoured such an approach as I think the decorative embellishments detract from the work's overall solemnity. I think I can be allowed to express such an opinion as *Messiah* has been part of me practically all my life! I am sure that most of the decorations which today are added in the name of authenticity also detract from the natural beauty of the themes so abundantly evident in almost ever bar.

Perhaps my finest recording will never be heard. In June 1946 I recorded the *Alleluia* from Bach's Cantata No. 51 which contains magnificent writing for solo soprano and trumpet obbligato. Once again I had to persuade Walter Legge to let me record it as in those days it was not considered a 'popular' title. Harry Mortimer was a natural choice as trumpeter and we both seemed in particularly fine fettle that day. When we heard the test pressing we were astonished and delighted with the results. Walter also enthused. We all considered it to be a real winner. Yet for reasons best known to himself Walter did not allow the side to be published. Neither Harry nor I had personal pressings and the master appears to have been destroyed. Many years later, not long before his unexpected death, I contacted Walter to see if he had salted away a pressing but he maintained in his reply that all his test records 'were at the bottom of Lake Geneva'. If true, some unsuspecting fisherman could be in for an unusual catch!

CHAPTER ELEVEN

Wartime Difficulties

IT IS time to pick up the threads of chronology once more. Apart
from two notable exceptions mentioned below, the basic tenor of
my life throughout the 1930s was very much according to the
pattern previously mentioned: a bulging engagement diary and a
great deal of travel!

One of the first big departures from my routine came in 1937
when I was invited to sing at Covent Garden during the International Coronation Season. The opera house management chose
to celebrate this with contrasted and varied repertoire including
Gluck's *Orfeo* in the expanded 1774 Paris version. This meant that
not only was the work sung in French but that the Ballet Company could also be involved. The original intention was that
Beecham should conduct André Burdino and Germaine Lubin in
the principal roles. It transpired that the latter was replaced, quite
gloriously as a matter of fact, by Maggie Teyte, and Beecham
withdrew late in the proceedings to be substituted by Fritz Reiner,
who had caused a very considerable stir with his Wagner performances the previous season. If my contribution was a modest
one – I sang just one song during the ballet – it was nevertheless
a supremely rewarding piece to sing and, hidden from view in
the orchestra pit, I could also view close-to the disciplinarian ways
of the great Reiner.

But undoubtedly the most startling change to my work came
in early 1939 when I was invited to participate in the 1940 New
Zealand Centennial Celebrations. When the Second World War
was declared just a few months later I had to face the fact that the
delightful prospect of an extended trip to New Zealand could

123

now be instantly forgotten. I was, therefore, both surprised and delighted when we were informed by the New Zealand authorities that if we were prepared to take the risk of travelling they would continue with their celebrations, albeit in modified form. We all readily agreed to take the chance particularly after the yawning inactivity which the arts underwent immediately after the outbreak of war. In the early stages of what was at that time so aptly called 'the phoney war' everything was cancelled – and I had had such a season mapped out in front of me! But gradually concerts were reinstated, though in order to skirt the difficulties of the blackout they were held at some unusual (particularly to a singer) hour of the day, so long as the audience could travel in daylight; sometimes as early as ten o'clock in the morning.

Eventually, on a cold March day in 1940 I left Britain for New Zealand sharing the easy, relaxed company of Gladys Ripley and Mr and Mrs Heddle Nash. Travelling via the Atlantic did prove rather unnerving; the ship was crowded with some six hundred or so refugees en route to America and at one point we were actually hit by a shell from a U-boat. Fortunately we were quick enough to escape further damage though two seamen were lost during this encounter. It was an incident which for some reason was kept extremely quiet and to this day I know very little about what actually happened. We also had to contend with a very rough crossing as we were in a flattish-bottomed boat originally intended to sail the calmer waters of the Mediterranean. When we called at Halifax in Nova Scotia I caught my first chilling sight of a submarine, a most unpleasant reminder of what had happened earlier in our voyage. Then we travelled down the coast to New York before completing a four-day train journey across the American continent. I also had the opportunity to stop with the rest of the party and proudly show them the Hollywood Bowl where I had sung with Harty in 1933. Then it was across the Pacific Ocean on the Matson Line calling in for just one day on my brother in Honolulu who entertained us most lavishly.

It proved a tonic to arrive in the quieter atmosphere of New Zealand. However I was keyed-up to wage a personal war for I had been 'tricked' by the small print in my contract and therefore had to appear in opera. I was determined, come what may, to wriggle out of such a prospect. Never in my wildest dreams did I contemplate singing in opera on stage; I just knew it was not for me. The size of my voice largely persuaded me that I was not cut out for the stage and besides, lingering in the back of my mind were the doubts I had always felt about opera as a musical art form: when I first started singing I had always rather grandly regarded opera as a hybrid form! But perhaps I was unfairly and unduly influenced by my earliest visits to the opera. In those days the singing was not especially good and I used to think of the acting as some kind of cover-up for bad singing. But my contract for New Zealand *did* contain references in the small print to performing Gounod's *Faust* which I admit to having totally overlooked. I made up my mind to withdraw from these operatic appearances, being quite determined to ask the authorities to replace me with someone from Australia. I quickly discovered, however, that our bass, Oscar Natzke, was apparently being difficult about appearing as Mefistofeles in such an out-of-the-way place as New Zealand, preferring to wait until he could appear, as he eventually and triumphantly did, either at Covent Garden or the New York Met in such a prestigious role. As a result there were several pre-performance meetings in order to solve these unexpected confusions, and when Professor Shelley, Music Director of the New Zealand Broadcasting Service and at this time overseer of the Centennial Celebrations, turned to me with a desperate look saying, almost menacingly it seemed, 'And I hope *you* are not going to try and get out of it!', all I could do was to melt with a feeble, 'Oh no! Of course not.'

Fortunately I knew the music from cover to cover having sung numerous concert performances of *Faust*, as well as seeing the opera on stage many times. I did have to resort to some homework, however, as there were no costumes. I consequently set to and consulted various reference books on historical costume before taking pencil to paper and designing Marguerite's gown. Every prop required in the opera also had to be made on the spot. I well remember the particularly stubborn jewel 'casket'. It looked absolutely superb but unfortunately the lid just would not stay open. When it came to the Jewel Song I was forced to hold the lid open with one hand and try on the jewels with the other – single handed jewel adornment is not the easiest of exercises! Things like that just did not happen in my quieter world of oratorio.

We took *Faust* to sixteen New Zealand towns and cities, garnering our chorus from the places where we toured but always secure and confident in the support provided by our own excellent orchestra. The eventual Mefistofeles was Raymond Beatty, at that time one of Australia's principal basses. Though he spent a few years in this country during, I believe, the late 1920s his career as a concert, operatic and oratorio singer was largely confined to his native Australia. Heddle, of course, was my handsome Faust with Gladys a convincing Siebel, looking most attractive in her high boots. The roles of Martha and Valentine were undertaken by young New Zealand singers. Our genial conductor was Anderson Tyrer. Anderson was originally trained as a pianist and conductor in Manchester; Ernest Newman dubbed him 'the high priest of polish in pianoforte playing'. His conducting studies were made under Michael Balling who took over the Hallé Orchestra from Hans Richter. Tyrer was also a composer and his symphonic poem for chorus, orchestra and orator, *Dr Faustus*, was performed several times during the celebrations. He later founded the New Zealand Symphony Orchestra. He was not the most authoritative conductor I have worked with though I personally never experienced any difficulties with him. I had a strong feeling that he relied heavily upon the leader of the orchestra, Maurice Clare, who proved a splendid companion. Maurice would walk me back to my hotel, criticising with commendable insight that evening's performance – 'Listen to the phrasing of the violin' he would repeatedly advise. I also recall how he once clarified for me a phrase in Delius's *Twilight Fancies*, a phrase which had long worried and baffled me. Maurice was also a connoisseur of wine and introduced me to some splendid examples from the world's finest vineyards. One night the company was favoured by the unexpected appearance of Sir Thomas Beecham who, en route to Australia, learnt of our presence and failed to resist the opportunity to conduct one of his all-time favourites.

Although I had not intended to sing in *Faust* on stage I have to admit to enjoying it thoroughly. It proved to be a particularly happy and rewarding experience and after those sixteen performances I felt I could have repeated the entire exercise all over again. Not having learnt the complicated skills of acting I simply relied upon my imagination which did not, apparently, let me down. One particular evening Heddle, always a tower of strength, was even moved to say, 'All your movements tonight were as smooth as silk' – perhaps I had gained some inspiration from a lifetime devoted to the movies.

Although Oscar Natzke had succeeded in wriggling out of

singing Mefistofeles he did join Heddle, Gladys and me for the many other appearances liberally sprinkled in between the *Faust* performances. Individual programmes would be drawn up for each town we visited; the larger the place the longer we stayed and the more we sang. In Christchurch, for example, besides appearing in *Faust* we also performed *Elijah*, Elgar's *King Olaf* and, in concert, *Carmen* (with Heddle as Don José, Gladys in the title role and myself as Micaëla) as well as some 'celebrity concerts'. Naturally we sang many *Messiah*s and *Creation*s wherever we went. Having sung *The Creation* alongside such a singer as Harold Williams, who invariably gave a superb performance, I was a little disturbed by Oscar's reading. He had not fully studied the part and was content merely to sing the notes. His performance consequently made no impact upon the audience. I think he realised he had not done his homework for after one performance when we returned to the green room Oscar threw his copy of the score across the room declaring, 'I'm never going to sing that again!' I could not resist the temptation to reply quietly, 'No, you shouldn't.' I received a daggers look but no retort. Oscar did have the ability to give a marvellous performance, though this was generally in the works he had studied with the great Garcia.

Wherever we went we were treated as VIPs, constantly chaperoned by government officials, with everything proceeding like some well-oiled, clockwork machine. Such treatment did incur, however, certain penalties, most notably the obligation to make little speeches wherever we went. I particularly remember a visit to a large school for boys in Wanganui where we were confronted by some eight hundred faces. The speeches began, first Heddle, then Oscar and myself; for some reason Gladys was left till last. She, however, prompted the loudest applause by the splendid one-liner: 'Well boys', she said, with a quite dazzling smile, 'I'm not used to making speeches; I'm much more used to talking to men one at a time!' Anyone who knew Gladys would appreciate the meaning behind that! She was a very vivacious and attractive girl and, needless to say, had the time of her life going over on the boat.

When the tour ended Gladys and I, each with a husband and daughter waiting for us at home, were anxious to return and so we left New Zealand in September much against the wishes of all those we had befriended in our happy sojourn there. Much was done to persuade us to stay, even to the extent of promising us

127

an engagement every night, but so determined were we to return to England that even these blandishments were vigorously resisted.

We travelled in the almost decadent luxury of the *SS Monterey*. At Tahiti we broke our journey for a single day. We were offered various conducted tours but we both opted to stay in Tahiti itself which at that time was little more than a colourful main street. I spent several contented hours gazing into a crystal clear sea where bright blue fish danced and darted. There were also some special displays put on by the Tahitian islanders. I watched them light a huge fire on to which they heaped quantities of large stones; as the fire blazed and the stones appeared to melt in the intense heat, so the islanders walked the twelve feet or so along these stones barefoot. When they stepped off at the other end their feet bore not a single mark nor did they display any evidence of discomfort. They also mounted an open air dramatisation of one of their legends. I have forgotten the details of this enactment but not the manner in which their dramatic 'curtain' was effected. Countless Tahitians carrying long painted shields would come on and form a vast concave line. Lifting their shields they would form a perfect screen. After the required change on stage had taken place they would depart sideways, the 'curtain' parting for the next scene. It was stunningly effective.

We then returned to Honolulu where I gave a recital in the Dillingham Hall, a far more romantic setting than the name implies. The hall itself was little more than a raised open stage but palm trees formed its perimeter and when singing one gazed up at the sky and stars. It was very inspiring, though I have to confess to being enormously assisted by my fine accompanist Verne Waldo Thompson who was head of the Conservatory of Music at Honolulu.

We then took the train from San Francisco to New York, making sure we did not miss the opportunity to sit in the parlour car where we could enjoy the spectacular panoramic views which surrounded us. On one such occasion we were joined by two gentlemen. After a while we were all engaged in conversation and one of our newly acquired companions asked Gladys where we were bound. 'Oh!', she replied, 'We're going home to England' – prompting the laughing reply, 'If there is any England left to go to!' My patriotic hackles were well and truly raised. 'Do you want to bet?' I interjected. He looked somewhat surprised

128

but agreed. 'All right, you put your name on this piece of paper and I'll bet you ten dollars that when we get back to England there will still be an England there!' I kept that piece of paper and when I returned wrote to him almost immediately although I didn't get my ten dollars. There is, however, a touching sequel to the story. Many years later I was giving a talk in Nottingham and told this story to my audience; afterwards a lady came up to me and pushed a ten dollar note into my hand saying, 'That's your ten dollars, I'd like you to have it.' She, an American, had honoured the bet after all.

By some miracle nothing untoward happened to our convoy journey from New York to England although when we arrived at Liverpool we saw that brave city being badly blitzed, its first heavy bombing of the war. From our sad vantage-point on deck we could see countless fires burning out of control. When we landed next morning Gladys and I sat for six hours or so on top of our luggage until a taxi could be found to take us to the station. Gladys successfully departed for London and I left for Manchester where I was met by my husband with the car. My first night home, however, was not to be a peaceful one: it was spent in the air raid shelter at the bottom of our garden as my return coincided with the night of Manchester's first big blitz. A land mine fell close by and the doors and windows of my home were blown in; a fine return to England. I wondered what I had come home to but wasn't at all sorry to be back! In common with just about everybody else in the British Isles one simply took a deep breath, gritted one's teeth and carried on.

In times of devastation and turmoil it is strange how the smaller, less significant details linger longest in the memory. I well recall around this time, arriving back in London during the depths of a blackout after singing on the East Coast. Groping my way out of the station with my bags I reached the street which, I discovered, had been badly bomb-damaged. In the pitch dark I took the inevitable tumble, hitting my eye on the ground in the process. Even as I fell I thought to myself how would I look next day, for I was due to sing at a special Royal Albert Hall concert organised to raise funds for the Russian allies. I awoke with a quite spectacular black eye, of course, and had to spend some considerable time in the make-up department so that at least I could look presentable; one has to try to look one's best when appearing on the stage of the Royal Albert Hall in front of an audience of more than nine thousand! Even more so when my colleagues were, on this occasion, Laurence Olivier and Peggy Ashcroft.

Not long after my return from New Zealand I was drawn into ENSA, the Entertainments National Service Association, which was being run by Walter Legge. ENSA's object was the organisation of recitals and concerts for troops and factories throughout the country. Like most of my colleagues, I gave countless performances at bases, camps and factories to enthusiastic and generous audiences, frequently at the instigation of the most cryptic, even furtive, instructions. A letter would, for example, baldly command, 'Go to the Liverpool Adelphi Hotel where a taxi will collect you at five o'clock. You will then be taken to somewhere in North Wales to give two concerts after which the taxi will return you to your hotel.' On that particular trip to 'somewhere in North Wales' I was actually taken inside a mountain where I found my audience, busy as bees, making munitions. To this day I don't know where it was.

The factory canteen was a very popular venue for the lunchtime recital. On one typical occasion I visited a factory in Birmingham and found the canteen laid out in what then appeared to be 'traditional' fashion with tables either side and a raised platform at one end. After the usual allowance of half-an-hour for lunch the employees were then given a brief recital. Nothing out of the ordinary in fact: until I read the startling headline to a review in the following day's local paper: 'Roast beef, two veg and Isobel Baillie'! These were the kind of places from which the BBC broadcast *Workers' Playtime*. How well I recall the overwhelming friendliness of such programmes. For the most part I sang my usual repertoire saving, perhaps, a few lighter songs for a happy, uncomplicated conclusion. As the audience appeared to enjoy what they were offered I saw no point in changing the contents or giving them watered-down fare.

Six weeks after the conclusion of the war in Europe I was put into uniform and sent off to the continent as a Second Lieutenant. My tour of duty included singing at the Palais des Beaux Arts in Brussels and at the Paris Leisure Centre in the Champs Elysées, the latter programme being shared with the famous French violinist, Jacques Thibaud, whose appearance was designed as a tribute to the British artists. We continued our travels, entertaining to the best of our ability the weary but victorious troops still in Europe. These naturally included men from the Common-wealth. One day I found myself at a Canadian camp. I was greeted by a huge Canadian who wrenched the car door open and com-menced to make a great fuss of me. What would I like? Just say the word and it would be mine! His face fell when I told him that the only thing I wanted at that moment was a cup of tea! 'I'm sorry, Ma'am', came the reply, 'We've no tea though there's plenty of champagne!' Later, on arriving at the drill hall to arrange a quick rehearsal, I noticed that the piano was bereft of its music stand. I innocently asked what had happened to the unfortunate stand. My bulky escort, somewhat embarrassed, shifted his weight and explained, 'Well Ma'am, you see the boys got so excited on VE day that they burnt it.' I still wonder how the rest of the instrument managed to escape a similar fate.

Slowly life returned to normal and the ENSA concerts wound up. They continued to be hard, difficult days, particularly while rationing was in force. Occasionally, however, there would be the unexpected and unsolicited present – I even had the offer of a 'food parcel' from a seven-year-old! I had promised a teacher friend of mine that I would sing at her school and the children were consequently subjected to a terrific build-up. Eventually they were asked to consider a suitable reward for my services. Apparently a little lad put up his hand generously exclaiming, 'Please Miss, I can bring a rabbit!' In those days that indeed would have been more than acceptable! Clothing also was severely ra-tioned and it was not an easy task to be suitably dressed when giving recitals and concerts; sometimes the manipulation of clothes coupons entailed far more effort than learning a score. Everything was exceptionally scarce. Once when travelling from Manchester to South Wales it even proved impossible to obtain that essential cup of tea anywhere. To make matters worse when I arrived at the hotel, absolutely gasping, I discovered the kitchen closed for the night. Not only did I go to bed desperately thirsty but also ravenously hungry. On the return journey I did, how-ever, discover a marvellous and quite infallible system. If the guard was informed well in advance that a cup of tea or some bread and butter would be welcome at a certain time, lo and behold!, it would be miraculously handed to me at the appointed station. What a joy that proved.

Throughout these troubled years Nancy had been working at the BBC. After a spell at Bristol, where many of the BBC's activities were transferred during the early stages of the war, she was brought back to London. A little later she took a job at Grosvenor Square with the United States Army from where she was transferred to the Office of the National Broadcasting Company. It was in a studio in the bowels of the Ministry of Information that she met Edward V. Roberts (Ned), then a war correspondent for the United Press.

Nancy and Ned were married in 1946. My first grandchild, Douglas Baillie Roberts, was born in 1948 and both Harry and I were thrilled and delighted. Sadly, Harry was never to see his granddaughter, Nancy Jennifer, born in 1958 only months after Harry's death.

CHAPTER TWELVE

Peace is Restored

HARRY's office was blitzed during the Second World War so he decided to retire early. Much to our surprise we found ourselves leaving Manchester in 1946 for the tranquillity and comparative seclusion of Selborne in Hampshire. The first two lines of the address will, I think, immediately convey the full atmosphere of the place – 'Trimmings, Gracious Street'. The love of the country, cultivated during our time at Silecroft, had far from deserted us and once again I could see that Harry was in his element, adoring every minute of his life, quietly gardening and entering into village life. Despite his failing health Harry's time at 'Trimmings' proved to be the happiest and most contented period of his existence. Selborne itself was, as it largely remains today, a delight, centred around the parish church with its ancient oak and its air of glorious peace. Naturally such a move meant slightly more commuting but I always felt it to be more than worth while once I had arrived home.

The move coincided with the early days of Nancy's marriage. Her home was now in Washington though Ned, now a member of the US Foreign Service, found himself in Paris for the United Nations General Assembly meeting, before the UN established itself in New York. Nancy's and Ned's close proximity just had to be taken advantage of and so they spent Christmas with us in Selborne before returning to the States.

With the worst of the post-war restrictions over I began my world travels again. Most of these wanderings were rooted in an attempt to visit Nancy and Ned who were now sampling many contrasting corners of the world as a result of Ned's work in the

American Foreign Service. My first trip abroad, however, resulted from an invitation in 1948 to return to New Zealand.

For the first time in my life I travelled by flying boat, a most exhilarating and comfortable experience. On landing in Singapore I was, much to my surprise, met by Adrian Holland who had played for me at concerts and recitals during the war in the UK. An Australian bound for his native country, he had spotted my name on the arrivals list in the local paper and come down to the docks to wait for me. There he stood with an invitation to give a recital that very evening. Always unable to resist the temptation to sing, I agreed and that night a more or less impromptu song recital was broadcast throughout Malaya. As a consequence I was asked if I would break my return journey and give more recitals which I was only too pleased to do.

My accompanist for the New Zealand tour was a native of that country, Wainright Morgan. It was Professor Shelley, the mastermind behind the Centennial Celebrations, who had suggested Mr Morgan. He was duly summoned to Wellington and after trying through a few songs with him I instantly knew that we could work together harmoniously. The next day we found ourselves travelling together on a train to an engagement. Mr Morgan produced Cornelia Otis Skinner's *Our Hearts were Young and Gay* to read. Having seen me laugh out loud several times over the book, he declared, 'I'm glad you laughed at that.' 'Why?' I enquired. 'Well, I didn't quite know how to approach you, but now I know exactly.' I thought it an ingenious way of breaking the ice and a subtle way of determining whether or not I had a sense of humour.

During the mid-1930s Wainwright came to London where he established himself as an accompanist for such singers as Dennis Noble, Norman Walker and Noel Eadie. He was also a composer and in 1937 his *Laughing Cavalier* was produced at the Adelphi Theatre. After serving with the RAF and the RNZAF he continued his musical life back in New Zealand. We worked in splendid accord. I attempted to provide a balanced programme for my audiences while varying them for myself so that I was kept fresh and on my toes. At Napier, for example, the programme opened with Arne's *O ravishing delight* and two Purcell numbers, *Dido's lament* and *Hark the echoing air*, before progressing to Handel's *Dearest of all men proven* and *He'll say that for love*. In a German *Lied* section there were Brahms's *To a nightingale*, *A love song* and

Sister dear followed by Schubert's *Who is Sylvia?* and *Gretchen at the spinning wheel*. The second half opened with Berlioz's *Absence* and *The unknown land* from *Les Nuits d'été* before proceeding to a group of songs by Richard Strauss, *Tomorrow*, *All Souls' Day* and *Serenade*. I closed with English music: Eric Fogg's *Peace*, Harty's *A lullaby* and *Lane o' the thrushes*, then Marjory Kennedy-Fraser's arrangements of *Kishmul's galley* and *A fairy's love song*.

Full of happy memories I left New Zealand and returned, as promised, to Malaya where I gave four recitals in Victoria Memorial Hall in Singapore. The programme of my Singapore 'farewell concert', accompanied by Adrian Holland, was very different from that just quoted, and quite a contrast, with only Arne's *O ravishing delight*, which opened the programme, duplicated. This baroque section continued with Bach's *Flocks in pastures green abiding*, Purcell's *Stript of their green* and Handel's *Art thou troubled?*. German *Lied* this time embraced Schubert's *The brook* and *Vital spark of heavenly flame* plus Grieg's *A dream*, *The princess* and *Last spring*. English music was then represented by Parry's *Where shall the lover rest?*, two songs by Wainwright Morgan (for I had been captivated by some of his little songs), *To music* and *Haste thee nymph*, Harty's *The stranger's grave* and Quilter's *Fair house of joy*. The final section, something of a pot-pourri, included Granados's *The maiden and the nightingale*, *The Wife of Bath* from Dyson's *The Canterbury Pilgrims*, Bantock's *The lament of Isis*, Hahn's *If my songs were winged*, Rutland Boughton's *Faery song* and Lady John Scott's *Think on me*.

I travelled up to Kuala Lumpur and Penang for further recitals. As there was no concert hall in Penang I sang in the Great Western Hotel, as I think it was called. Much to my surprise I there discovered a friend whom I had first met during the war at Warrington where I had been singing to the troops. Jane Brown-Sanders had by this time married and now assisted her husband in the running of the Penang Broadcasting Station. They were ideal people for showing me the locale. I was taken into the forests to visit a school run by missionary nuns who proudly displayed their large communal hall. My accompanist, also enjoying the pleasure trip, started to play my songs and so I began to sing. Before long all the open windows were crowded with little wide-eyed faces peering silently through. I was also taken to a native encampment where I was invited to dine with the chief and his wives. Nothing ventured nothing gained. I sat with him and modestly partook of their meal which had the colour and consistency of mud. I was later told that my politeness had guaranteed that I could be buried anywhere I wanted within their territory when the time came!

My next major visit was to Washington DC, USA which was now Nancy's home. It was ostensibly planned as a family visit though once again I ended up singing. Nancy had become friendly with most of Washington's musical inhabitants including Paul Callaway, organist and choirmaster of Washington Cathedral. When she mentioned that I was going to visit her he enquired whether I would consider singing for him in the cathedral. Nancy's reply, 'You only have to ask her', resulted in my singing in that most beautiful building, in atmosphere not unlike Gloucester Cathedral, on 3 July 1949. To Paul Callaway's most sensitive accompaniment I sang Bach's *Flocks in pastures green abiding*, Handel's *Let the bright seraphim* (to a brilliant trumpet obbligato from Lloyd Geister, the first trumpet of the Washington National Symphony Orchestra) and *The sun goeth down* from Elgar's *The Kingdom*.

Much to everyone's surprise the congregation for this Sunday concert after Evensong was exceptionally large. I discovered that this was because Paul Hume, music critic of the *Washington Post*, had mentioned the forthcoming recital in his column. He had, it appeared, long been a fan of my records and in his resultant review wrote most flatteringly that this 'was one of the finest concerts of the year' and that 'we must hope to hear Isobel Baillie again while she is visiting this country', an entreaty which was not forgotten.

In 1953 I left the United Kingdom once more, this time for a recital tour of South Africa. I flew by the then much heralded Comet (later grounded after much controversy) and gave concerts in towns and cities dotted across the vast stretches, among them Nairobi, Salisbury, Johannesburg, Cape Town, Durban and Grahamstown. Many maintain that world travel is wearying but I have never minded it, generally taking it in my stride and enjoying every moment. I have to admit to having had a marvellous time in South Africa. I arranged my programmes with great care, making sure that they were acceptable to all kinds of listeners.

The hall in which I sang in Nairobi was a most beautiful place, but there is an even sharper memory attached to it than the elegant proportions of the hall: when I came out onto the platform to commence my recital I discovered that I could hardly breathe. Being six thousand feet or so above sea level made itself very apparent. Fortunately, though, I was able to make a hasty adjustment by taking far deeper breaths than normal, thus securing more oxygen, which enabled me to carry off the performance. Apart from recitals I also had the pleasure of some concert work with the orchestras of Johannesburg, Cape Town and Durban.

During the time I was staying in Nairobi the Mau Mau were being particularly troublesome! On my arrival I was taken to the Norfolk Hotel and accommodated in a suite entirely separate from the hotel situated some way along the road. The room was overflowing with exotic flowers and there were two kind ladies to attend to my every need. I was, however, taken aback when one of them looked at me in a most serious manner and said, 'Now Miss Baillie, after you have had your bath and have changed ready to go to the hotel for dinner just pick up the phone and ask for an escort.' I naïvely asked why I should possibly require an escort, insisting that I was quite capable of walking the few yards involved by myself. The warning was, however, repeated and in the cause of a peaceful co-existence I agreed. Then the second lady enquired, 'You do lock your door at night don't you Miss Baillie?' 'Oh yes', I replied, 'Always in a place like this.' But after all the veiled warnings and unusual precautions I hardly slept that night. It was consequently with much relief that the following day I encountered the familiar face of an old friend, once a singer in London and now living in Nairobi with her husband. It did not take much enticement on her part to persuade me to substitute the uneasy atmosphere of the Norfolk Hotel for the home comforts of their house in Muthaga. She did mention that they kept Kikuyu servants but that they were locked out at night. Save for the incessant noise of the frogs my night's sleep was at last untroubled. It was not until a little later that I discovered I had been much nearer the dreaded Mau Mau at Muthaga than I had been at the Norfolk Hotel!

Before I left Nairobi for Salisbury I was asked if I would give a broadcast. Once again I readily agreed. On arriving at the Broadcasting Station some ten miles or so from the city centre I was met by the Station Director who, I noticed with some surprise, was wearing a gun at his belt. After the introductory formalities I also discovered that not only was the announcer wearing a gun but so was the lady accompanist! I was feeling rather tired, for Nairobi had proved a most sociable city, so sitting in the green room waiting to go into the studio I attempted to summon up as much adrenalin as I could muster. It seemed desperately important for here I was surrounded by all those guns: 'My word', I thought to myself, 'I had better sing well tonight!'

My last planned engagement in South Africa was a recital in the Johannesburg Art Gallery. However, once again I was asked to slot in an extra concert, this time for a very different audience. My accompanist asked me if I would go with him to the Bantu Centre and sing there. It was not a particularly large audience but it was highly appreciative. I will never forget two little girls in the front row who, whenever I took a high, soft note would open their eyes wide, look up and clasp their hands as if in prayer, softly murmuring 'Ahhhh!' My reward for singing was a quite lovely picture of a kraal. Several people who have subsequently written books about the Bantu have mentioned my visit.

I first went to Hong Kong in 1970 in order to adjudicate at their competitive music festival. On my way I took the opportunity to make a diversion to India at the invitation of the Second Secretary of the British Consulate in Madras, where I sang and gave the talk about my life which I had by then added to my repertoire. I was well entertained and even took tea on those famous lawns. I also expressed a wish to see Calcutta though was asked by my host to reconsider such a venture, well-intentioned advice designed to spare me the horrors of the agonising poverty experienced on all sides in that unfortunate city. It was, however, advice which had to be ignored for my Comet to Hong Kong departed from Calcutta. Calcutta is undoubtedly not a place to visit if one has a heart; the poverty was too awful for words. When I eventually arrived in Hong Kong not only did I discover that the competition was enormous, certainly the largest I have ever adjudicated, but that I was also expected to sing and give my talk. The masterclasses were very demanding but particularly interesting, though I prefer one-to-one contact. The chief difficulty of a masterclass is keeping everyone fully involved. In smaller, intimate classes the students can ask questions and participate to a far greater level.

I also treasure memories of a visit to Korea, a trip funded by Korea's main newspaper and which came about as the result of a telegram from the same Second Secretary, now at the British

Embassy in Korea, who had heard that I intended visiting my brother in Honolulu and who wondered if I would be prepared to extend my journey and spend some time there. I accepted and subsequently spent a superb month in Korea. Besides the usual recitals I also broadcast on radio and television, sang some sacred arias in Seoul Cathedral and gave some masterclasses. My trip to Japan also proved memorable, the undoubted highlight being an impromptu invitation to sing in St Alban's Church in Tokyo. I have always enjoyed singing in cathedrals, the sound floating on the vast, open space never failing to excite me. After singing there I was given the most beautiful brooch, a large single pearl surrounded by emeralds, by the English businessman who had invited me to sing. Also, for some reason the officiating clergyman could hardly believe that the Isobel Baillie he knew in England could suddenly appear in the middle of Tokyo! While in Tokyo I attended concerts given by a remarkable young boy conductor named Seiji Ozawa who, during the interval, would come and mingle with the audience. I have followed his amazing career with interest ever since.

Although my travels started comparatively late in my career I certainly made up for lost time!

Epilogue

THERE comes a point in every singer's life when the march of
time has to be squarely faced. After all no singer can go on
forever. Some opt for an abrupt and total withdrawal from concert life, others for a more gradual wind-up. I chose the latter
course and am, to some extent, still in the process of curtailing
my activities. (They will probably only entirely cease when I do!)

Even in the 1950s some friends began to mention that it was
'remarkable' that I should still be singing in my mid- and late
fifties, an age when sopranos are apparently supposed to be past
their best and transported to statutory pastures of retirement. I
believed, however, that age has little to do with singing and
provided my voice sounded (to my ears) 'right' then it remained
all systems go. Much of this is, of course, an attitude of mind; I
think it is quite possible to sound young and fresh even in one's
fifties. Naturally I realised that my career had to follow a different
path from that taken in the 1930s and 40s but the changes and
modifications were very gradual, almost imperceptible, and took
a surprising number of years, ten or so at least. I had, in fact,
initiated the process myself as long ago as the war years when I
made the decision not to sing the Hallé *Messiah* again. Perhaps
the full realisation that I could not indefinitely go on singing
professionally came when I received that letter from Dr Sumsion
after the 1955 Three Choirs Festival in which he explained that
he felt it was now time to let someone else 'have a go'. Each
withdrawal was undertaken after much thought and consideration. The uppermost thought as I faced each decision was the
desire to take my leave while still at my best in a particular work,

140

a decision which arose out of my respect for the music rather than an inability to face its technical challenge. After withdrawing from the Hallé *Messiah* the time came to resign from other 'traditional' *Messiahs*; that with the Royal Choral Society after thirty-three performances, as well as the Royal Edinburgh Choral Society after more than twenty appearances, and in recognition of which they made me a Vice President of their Society. I continued to sing *Messiah* in other places for many years, much depending on how comfortable I felt in each specific venue. Some works I have never stopped singing: *The Creation* and *Elijah*, for example. I gave my most recent performance of *Elijah* when I was eighty, agreeing to sing the soprano part at a performance in Radlett in order to bolster the confidence of a pupil of mine who had been engaged to sing the tenor role. I would sing it again if the opportunity arose for I have never given a farewell performance and certainly do not intend to.

So, by the mid-1950s the emphasis had begun to shift and the pattern of my life now embraced both singing and teaching, the latter gradually taking the upper hand. I had taken a few private pupils as early as the late 1940s as I believed teaching to be an invaluable method by which to pass on the knowledge and insight acquired during a lifetime at one's craft. Teaching can also be richly rewarding if highly demanding. I will always remember Ivor Newton's remark when he learnt that I was going to teach at the Royal College of Music. He looked me straight in the eye and said, 'Isobel, I've played for countless celebrities for over sixty years, most of whom turned to teaching – yet they gave nothing!' I hope I might be an exception to Ivor's sad reflection.

I first started to teach at the Royal College of Music in 1952, I think it was. The invitation came from Sir George Dyson, then still head of the RCM, after that previously mentioned performance of his *The Canterbury Pilgrims* at the Royal Albert Hall. I was not keen at first as I had never been seriously attached to a college or school at any time during my singing career but it was something new and a challenge which, I hardly need add, greatly appealed to me. I was there about three years when I was more or less obliged to withdraw owing to the declining state of Harry's health. I felt I wanted to spend as much time with him as possible, especially as there were still so many engagements coming in from all parts of the British Isles keeping me away from home a great deal. It happened that I was actually teaching at the RCM when the news came, via the telephone, that he had died suddenly at his beloved 'Trimmings'. Nancy felt, as I did, that Harry's 'home', however, was Manchester and so after a Requiem Holy Communion early in the morning at Selborne I made the long, sad journey to Manchester where the cremation took place.

After Harry's death I decided that the best course of action was to continue the schedule of hard work; a great antidote to practically all troubles. Rather than teach I chose to continue my world travels as there were so many open and standing invitations from earlier years. I had by no means shaken off the travel bug, and it consequently did not take a great deal of effort to pack my cases once more. I revisited Asia, Africa and America, teaching, adjudicating and singing. Such jaunts have not ceased. Although my last around-the-world trip was in 1965, I still regularly cross the Atlantic – one of the perks of having a daughter in Florida and grandchildren and great-grandchildren in other parts of that perennially exciting country.

I stayed in America for an entire year in 1960–61 when I took up an extended teaching engagement as Professor of Singing at the Department of Music at Cornell University. It's campus was gloriously positioned by the waters of Five Fingers Lake in New York State, and in this majestic setting I was given a splendid apartment and each evening ate my meal at the University Hotel School. In all respects it proved a most memorable stay. The majority of students did not wish to become professional singers but were there simply because of their love of music and their wish to learn as much as they could about the subject. The English repertoire was largely uncharted territory to them and they thrilled to the songs of Purcell and Arne as eagerly as to Elgar, Vaughan Williams and Finzi. The latter's *Dies natalis* made a quite remarkable impression. I had intended singing just one movement from the work at a recital but during a rehearsal my accompanist, the resident Professor of Music, John Fitzpatrick, insisted that the *entire* work must be sung. I even included some of the ballads of yesteryear as I firmly believe that a singer who can sing a ballad can turn his voice and interpretative talents to almost anything.

I took over from Keith Falkner who had been on the faculty for the previous ten years. It was Keith who was instrumental in securing my appointment there. During his final year, unbeknown to me he had apparently mentioned my name to the administration and played them some of my recordings which

142

had, I later discovered, been heard and enjoyed. To this day I do not know why Keith put forward my name. We were not exceptionally close friends though we had, of course, long been working colleagues. Perhaps he liked my work. I had to agree to stay just a year though after I had been there six weeks the authorities were anxious for me to stay much longer. Despite their protests I decided to return to Britain once the year had elapsed. Much as I was enjoying my stay I knew I would need the company and companionship of my friends at home once twelve months had passed.

On my return from Cornell I was asked by Keith, then Principal of the RCM, if I would support him there for a while. He asked me to return for a year but I insisted that it should be for three years or none at all as it would be unfair for the pupils, most of whom undergo a three-year period of study, to have a change of tutor in mid-stream. By this time I had also been teaching, as and when my commitments allowed, over a number of years at the Manchester School of Music run by John Grierson and William Taylor. With my eventual move back to Manchester in the mid-1970s I was able to devote even more time to the Manchester school. I still continue to teach there, though now for just a few special pupils, one of whom is Caroline Foster. A violinist who has played with many of this country's major orchestras, she also possesses a most beautiful natural contralto voice and well deserves the reputation she has made for herself in the North.

I also have some 'special' London pupils, Dinah Harris for example, who was first brought to me by her mother, Sylvia (one of my first ever pupils) in order to go through the *Messiah* solos for a school concert. By way of an introduction to her voice Dinah chose to sing, quite enchantingly as it transpired, a little French song. There and then I informed Sylvia, 'This girl is undoubtedly a singer!' On leaving school Dinah came to me before furthering her studies with Rita Streich, the foremost German coloratura soprano of her generation. Among my male pupils Charles Corp is undoubtedly one to watch out for. When he first came to me for an audition several years ago I spotted what I thought was potentially a fine lyric tenor voice. In those early stages the voice was, naturally, a little rough and there was much to learn but after some initial coaching he gained an entry into the Guildhall School of Music and was soon winning prizes. I always place emphasis on an all-round musical education as it is something I myself went without. I had no formal music lessons and even had to teach myself how to read music.

My ear for spotting talent is, not, however, confined to my own pupils. I well remember adjudicating at the RCM some years ago when a young baritone came forward and sang an extract from Britten's *Billy Budd* – a most adventurous choice. I immediately felt that here was something very special and despite some initial opposition from my colleagues on the panel I stuck to my guns and awarded him first place. His name was Thomas Allen, now one of this country's finest baritones. Outstanding singers must have a voice plus. That 'plus' is almost impossible to define, call it personality, charisma or what you will, but a voice without that 'plus', no matter how stupendous it is, will only ever be a voice.

Just as I thought the rest of my days would be spent teaching, out of the blue came yet another challenge – talks. The thought of talking about my life and work had until then never occurred to me. Although I knew I could sing to an audience I was far from certain that I could *talk* to one. It all came about when I received an invitation from the Liverpool Philharmonic Club, for whom I had sung on many occasions, asking me if I would care to tell them the story of my life. I began to draw up the rough outlines of a talk though I have to admit to not realising the amount of preparation such an undertaking would involve. Eventually I came up with the framework of an illustrated talk which I have subsequently given on literally hundreds of occasions in all parts of the country as well as various assorted corners of the world. From the start I have always tried to illustrate my talk, entitled 'Second Best', with some of the songs that have been with me all my life. This I still do though I now choose the songs very carefully – at my age it is a privilege in which I can indulge!

During the past twenty years or so my accompanist has invariably been John Grierson of the Manchester School of Music who has always proved to be the proverbial tower of strength. The quotation from Hilaire Belloc which opened these musings and reflections impinged itself upon my mind from the moment of our first encounter a forgotten number of years ago

> The best of all trades is to make songs
> And the second best is to sing them.

For over eighty years now, over sixty of them professionally, I have been doing 'second best'. What has proved so unexpected, so marvellous and so rewarding has been the way I have enjoyed my trade. I can in all honesty claim to have loved 'second best' – strange as such a statement might initially appear.

All my life I have striven to do my best in the only trade I truly know. Any success I might have enjoyed resulted from the kindness of those who mattered most, the audience. They are the ultimate judges. All I can do is to thank my loyal and long-devoted friends from my innermost depths for the love and kindness they have shown for so long.

It has been a wonderful life and I would do it all again!

APPENDIX A

Repertoire List

THE following provides an outline of Isobel Baillie's repertoire. The language used for each title indicates the language in which that work was generally sung.

CR indicates a composition premièred by Isobel Baillie.

ARDITI
Il bacio

ARNE
Comus: When daisies pied
The judgement of Paris: O
    ravishing delight
The tempest: Where the bee sucks

J. S. BACH
Cantatas (majority of)
Christmas Oratorio
Come sweetest death
Comfort sweet
In faith I quiet wait
Magnificat in D
Mass in B minor
St John Passion
St Matthew Passion

BACH/GOUNOD
Ave Maria

BALFE
The bohemian girl: I dreamt that
    I dwelt in marble halls

BALLADS
A birthday
A May morning
Among the willows
An old garden
At the mid-hour of night
Down in the forest
Do you believe in fairies
Easter flowers
I love the moon
I think
Melisande in the wood
My dearest heart
One morning very early
Sea rapture
Smile of spring
So we'll go no more a-roving
Spring's awakening
Still as the night
Three green bonnets
Willow song

BANTOCK
Home thoughts
Lament of Isis

BAX
I heard a piper piping
The white peace

BEETHOVEN
Choral Fantasy
Choral Symphony

BERLIOZ
Childhood of Christ
Damnation of Faust (Marguerite)
Nuits d'été
The Trojans

BESLY
Song in loneliness

BISHOP
Bid me discourse
Should he upbraid

BIZET
Carmen (Micaëla)

BLISS
Pastoral: Pigeon song

BOUGHTON
The immortal hour: Faery song

BRAHMS
A love song
Constancy
Faint and fainter is my slumber
Fruitless serenade
German Requiem
In summer fields
O forest cool
The sandman
Serenade
Sister dear
Swallow from over the sea
Sweet melodies
To a nightingale

BRENT SMITH
Elegy (CR)

BRIDGE
E'en as a lovely flower
Go not, happy day
Love went a-riding
O that it were so
So early in the morning o'

BRUCH
Ave Maria

G. BUSH
In praise of Mary (CR)

CADMAN
At dawning
From the land of the sky blue
  water

CASELLA
The Venetian convent

COSTA
Eli: I will extol thee

DARKE
Hymn of heavenly beauty

DAVID
La perle du Brésil: Charming
  bird

DAVIES
When childer plays

DEBUSSY
The blessed damozel
L'enfant prodigue: Air de Lia

DELIUS
In the Seraglio gardens
Love's philosophy
The nightingale

Twilight fancies
Venevil

DIACK
Creep afore you gang
Feetikins
Wee Willie Winkie

DUNHILL
The cloths of heaven

DVOŘÁK
Biblical songs: nos 4, 5 and 10
Rusalka: O silvery moon
Songs my mother taught me
The spectre's bride: Where art
    thou, father dear?
Te deum

DYSON
The Canterbury Pilgrims (CR)
Quo Vadis (CR)

ELGAR
The Apostles
King Olaf
The Kingdom
Like to the damask rose
Queen Mary's song
Sea pictures: Where corals lie
The spirit of England: For the
    fallen

FAURÉ
Après un rêve
Clair de lune
Requiem

FINZI
Dies natalis

FOGG
Carol of the little king
The dove

In service
Jesukin
One morning in a flower garden
Peace
Songs of the little folk
Spindrift
Summer song
To morning

FRANZ
Love's sanctuary

FULTON
Three songs with string quartet
    (CR)

GERMAN
Charming Chloë
Merrie England
Tom Jones

GIBBS
Ann's cradle song
In the woods in June
Joan of Arc: song cycle (CR)
Love is a sickness
Sailing homeward
To one who passed whistling
    through the night

GLUCK
Paris et Helena: O del mio dolce
    ardor

GOUNOD
Faust (Marguerite)

GRANADOS
The Maja and the nightingale

M. GREEN
O praise the Lord

GRIEG
A dream

A swan
The first primrose
From Monte Pincio
I love thee
Last spring
Peer Gynt: Solveig's song; Cradle
 song
The princess
With a waterlily

GURNEY
Carol of the Skiddaw jowes
Desire in spring
Down by the salley gardens
Hawk and buckle
Nine o' the clock o'
Orpheus
Severn meadows
Sleep
Sowing
Spring
Tears
Under the greenwood tree
You are my sky

HAGEMAN
At the well
Christ went up into the hills
Do not go, my love

HAHN
If songs were only winged

HANDEL
Acis and Galatea
Alessandro: Ne' trionfi
 d'Alessandro . . . Lusinghe più
 care
Amadigi di Gaula: Joy come to
 my breast
Israel in Egypt
Joshua
Judas Maccabaeus
Messiah

Ode for St Cecilia's day
Rodelinda: Art thou troubled?
Samson
Saul
Semele: O sleep, why dost thou
 leave me?
Solomon
Theodora: Angels ever bright and
 fair
Xerxes: Dearest of all men
 proven; He'll say that for my
 love; Largo; Marble my heart is
 . . . Flawless as noonday

HARRISON
Harvest Cantata (CR)

HARTY
Across the door
A lullaby
By the bivouac's fitful flame
The children of Lir (CR)
Cradle song
Grace for light
Herrin's in the bay (Antrim &
 Donegal)
Hush song
Lane o' the thrushes
Ode to a nightingale
The scythe song
Sea wrack
The stranger's grave
The two houses, etc.

HAYDN
Coronation Mass
The Creation
The mermaid's song
My mother bids me bind my hair
The sailor's song
The seasons
She never told her love
The spirit's song

HEAD
A blackbird singing
The fairies dance
The happy wanderer
Sweet almond blossom
Sweet chance, that led my steps
  abroad
Weathers (CR)

HILDASH
The minstrel

HOLST
Four songs for voice and violin,
  Op.35
The heart worships
Twelve songs, Op.48

HOWELLS
Come sing and dance
Gavotte
Hymnus paradisi (CR)
In greenways
The old house
Under the greenwood tree

M. HULL
Loveliest of trees (CR)

IRELAND
The heart's desire
If there were dreams to sell
I have twelve oxen
The lent lily
Spring sorrow, etc.

KJERULF
Synnöve's song

KODALY
Budavari Te deum
Missa brevis (CR)★

★CR of revised version made for
  1948 Three Choirs Festival

KORBAY
My brown boy

LA FORGE
To a messenger

LEONCAVALLO
I pagliacci: Ballatella; Nedda/
  Silvio duet

LEROUX
Le nil

LIE
Soft-footed snow

LISZT
Liebestraum
The Lorelei
Oh! quand je dors

MALUSKIN
O could but my song tell my
  sorrow

MASCAGNI
Cavalleria rusticana (Santuzza)

MENDELSSOHN
Elijah
Greeting
Hear my prayer . . . O for the
  wings of a dove
Hymn of praise
I would that my love
On wings of song
St Paul
42nd Psalm

MORGAN
Haste thee, nymph
To music

MOZART
A questo seno deh vieni

Ah, lo previdi
Contentment
Exsultate, jubilate
La finta giardiniera: A maiden's is
  an evil plight
Forget-me-not
The magician
The marriage of Figaro: O come
  do not delay; Thou, o love;
  You who have knowledge;
  Vanish'd are ye
Mass in C minor
Requiem
My heart in my bosom
Il re pastore: Thine shall I be for
  ever!
The seraglio: I leave you, but bid
  you beware
To solitude
Ye who the great creator . . . Lo
  in these works

OFFENBACH
Tales of Hoffmann (Olympia,
  Giulietta, Antonia and Stella)

PARRY
Crabbed age and youth
Judith: scenes
Where shall the lover rest?
Whether I live

PERGOLESI
Stabat mater

PUCCINI
La bohème: Lovely maid in the
  moonlight; Mimi's arias
Madam Butterfly: Love duet;
  One fine day
Tosca: Love and music

PURCELL
The blessed virgin's expostulation

Come ye sons of art: Sound the
  trumpet
Dido and Aeneas (Belinda);
  Dido's lament
Evening hymn
The fairy queen: Hark! the
  echoing air; Mystery's song;
  When I have often heard
The Indian Queen: Let us wander
I saw that you were grown so
high
King Arthur: Fairest Isle;
  Shepherd, cease decoying
The knotting song
The Libertine: Nymphs and
  shepherds
Stript of their green our groves
  appear
Where shall the lover rest?

QUILTER
Blackbird's song
Blow, blow thou winter wind
Fair house of joy
The fuchsia tree
Love's philosophy
Now sleeps the crimson petal
Over the mountains
To daisies

RACHMANINOV
Before my window
The bells
Christ is risen
Lilacs
The little island
My lovely maiden
No prophet I!
The soldier's wife
Sorrow in springtime
Spring waters
To the children
Vocalise

RAVEL
Schéhérazade

RIMSKY-KORSAKOV
The golden cockerel: Hymn to
  the sun
May night: Song of India
The rose enslaves the nightingale
Snow maiden: Lel's song

ROOTHAM
Ode on the morning of Christ's
  nativity (CR)

SAINT-SAËNS
Le bonheur est chose légère

SANDERSON
A birthday
When the moon swings low

A. SCARLATTI
Sento nel core

SCHUBERT
Ave Maria
The birds
The brook
First loss
Gretchen at the spinning wheel
Hark! hark! the lark
In spring
Laughter and wine
Love's message
Lullaby
Night and dreams
On the water
Pigeon post
Rosamunde: Romance
Rose bud red
The secret
Shepherd on the rock
Seligkeit
Serenade
Suleika's song
Thou art my rest
To a nightingale
To music

The trout
Vital spark of heavenly flame
Who is Sylvia?
Young man, etc.

SCHUMANN
A little folk song
The chestnut tree
Das verlassne Mägdelein
Du bist wie eine Blume
Frauenliebe und Leben
Frühlingsnacht
Hope
Ladybird
Liebesbotschaft
The lotus flower
Lovely month of May
Marienwürmchen
Moonlight
Nur wer die Sehnsucht kennt
The snowdrop
Snowflakes
The star
Stille Thränen, etc.

C. SCOTT
Blackbird's song
Daffodils
Don't come in, Sir, please
From afar
Have you seen him pass by?
Invocation
Lullaby

LADY J. SCOTT
Annie Laurie
Think on me

M. SHAW
The cuckoo
Heffle-cuckoo fair
Song of the palanquin bearer

SIBELIUS
Black roses

SINDING
Sylvelin

SMYTH
The wreckers: selected arias
Mass in D

SPEAKS
Morning
Sylvia

SPOHR
The last judgement
Rose, softly blooming

STANFORD
A soft day

STÖLZEL (attrib.)
Be thou with me

STORACE
The pretty creature

O. STRAUS
My hero

R. STRAUSS
All mein Gedanken
All souls' day
Devotion
Dream in the twilight
Night
Say wherefore
Serenade
Tomorrow
Wiegenlied, etc.

SULLIVAN
The golden legend
Orpheus with his lute

SZYMANOWSKI
Stabat mater

TCHAIKOVSKY
At the ball
Believe it not
Legende
None but the weary heart
The Princess
Tears
Was I not a blade of grass?
Why?

TOSELLI
Serenade

TOSTI
Goodbye
Parted

TOYE
Miranda

TRADITIONAL
A fairy's love song
Afton water
A joyous Easter hymn
An Eriskay love lilt
A rosebud by my early walk
Came ye by Athol
Ca' the yowes to the knowes
Comin' thro' the rye
Duncan Gray
The flowers of the forest
Gallant weaver
Have you seen but a whyte lily
   grow
I'm ower young to marry yet
I will walk with my love
John Anderson, my Joe
The Kerry dance
Kishmull's galley
O can ye sew cushions
O leave your sheep
O open the door
O whistle an' I'll come to ye
Robin Adair

Skye boat song
Snowy breasted pearl
Turn ye to me
Ye banks and braes, etc.

VAUGHAN WILLIAMS
Benedicite
Dona nobis pacem
Let beauty awake
Mass in G minor
Orpheus with his lute
Pastoral Symphony
Sea Symphony
Serenade to music (CR)
Silent noon
Song of thanksgiving

VERDI
Aida: Aida's aria
Otello: Ave Maria; Willow song
Requiem

WAGNER
The Flying Dutchman: Senta's
    ballad
Götterdämmerung: finale
Lohengrin (Elsa)
Die Meistersinger: Quintet
Tannhäuser: Elizabeth's greeting
    and Elizabeth's prayer

Tristan: Act 2, Liebestod
Walküre: finale

WALLACE
Maritana: Scenes that are
    brightest

WALTON
Through gilded trellises

WARLOCK (arr.)
Elizabethan songs with string
    quartet
Pretty ring time

WILSON
Carmena

WOLF
Er ist's
The forgotten maiden
Mausfallan Sprüchlein
Nun wandre Maria
Secrecy
St Nepomuks Vorabend

WOODFORDE-FINDEN
Indian love lyrics

WOODMAN
A birthday

Three Choirs Festival Appearances

* conducted by the composer
† first performance

1929: Worcester

13 September Cathedral	Handel: Messiah (w. Millicent Russel/Hubert Eisdell/Keith Falkner)

1931: Gloucester

9 September Shire Hall	Howells: In greenways*
11 September Cathedral	Handel: Messiah (w. Margaret Severn/Heddle Nash/ Harold Williams)

1932: Worcester

8 September Cathedral	Vaughan Williams: Benedicite* Elgar: For the fallen* Haydn: Creation, Part 1 (w. Francis Russell/Keith Falkner)
9 September Cathedral	Handel: Messiah (w. Percy Manchester/Gladys Ripley/Harold Williams)

1934: Gloucester

4 September Cathedral	Mozart: Requiem (w. Mary Jarred/Trefor Jones/ Keith Falkner)
5 September Cathedral	Bach: Magnificat in D (w. Elsie Suddaby/Mary Jarred/Trefor Jones/Keith Falkner)
6 September Cathedral	Rootham: Ode on the morning of Christ's Nativity* (w. Trefor Jones/Roy Henderson)

1935: Worcester

5 September Cathedral	Elgar: The Apostles (w. Astra Desmond/Heddle Nash/William Parsons/Roy Henderson/Harold Williams)
6 September Cathedral	Handel: Messiah (w. Mary Jarred/Heddle Nash/Harold Williams)

1936: Hereford

8 September Cathedral	Elgar: The Apostles (w. Astra Desmond/Heddle Nash/Keith Falkner/Roy Henderson/William Parsons)
11 September Cathedral	Handel: Judas Maccabæus (extracts) Handel: Messiah, 'Four scenes'[1] (w. Edward Reach/William Parsons)

1937: Gloucester

9 September Cathedral	Kodály: Budavari Te Deum★ Verdi: Requiem (both w. Mary Jarred/Heddle Nash/Keith Falkner)
10 September Cathedral	Parry: Judith (scenes) (w. Edward Reach/Harold Williams) Handel: Messiah (extracts) (w. Astra Desmond/Edward Reach/Harold Williams)

1938: Worcester

6 September	Fauré: Requiem (w. Harold Williams)
9 September Cathedral	Darke: Hymn of heavenly beauty★ (w. Roy Henderson) Handel: Saul, Pt 3 (w. Roy Henderson/Harold Williams/Mary Jarred/Edward Reach) Handel: Messiah (extracts) (w. Mary Jarred/Heddle Nash/Harold Williams)

1939[2]: Hereford

5 September Cathedral	Elgar: The Kingdom (w. Astra Desmond/Heddle Nash/Harold Williams) Brent Smith: Elegy (w. Harold Williams)
6 September The Kemble	A concert which was to have included Isobel Baillie singing Isolde's Narration (Wagner)
7 September Cathedral	Dyson: Quo Vadis? (w. Astra Desmond/Heddle Nash/Roy Henderson) Vaughan Williams: Dona nobis pacem (w. Roy Henderson)

1940–45 No Festivals held

1946: Hereford

10 September Cathedral	Elgar: The Kingdom (w. Astra Desmond/Heddle Nash/George Pizzey) Brent Smith: Elegy†★ (w. George Pizzey)
11 September The Kemble	A concert in which Isobel Baillie sang The Wife of Bath (Dyson: The Canterbury Pilgrims) and L'amerò sarò costante (Mozart)
12 September Cathedral	Dyson: Quo Vadis?, Pt 1†★ (w. Astra Desmond/ Heddle Nash/George Pizzey) Vaughan Williams: Benedicite

1947: Gloucester

9 September Cathedral	Elgar: The Apostles (w. Mary Jarred/Eric Greene/ Henry Cummings/Gordon Clinton/Harold Williams) Dyson: Quo Vadis?, Pt 1★ (w. Gladys Ripley/ Heddle Nash/Norman Walker)

1948: Worcester

7 September Cathedral	Elgar: The Kingdom (w. Mary Jarred/Heddle Nash/ Harold Williams) Szymanowski: Stabat mater (w. Mary Jarred/Harold Williams)
9 September Cathedral	Kodály: Missa brevis★ (w. Ena Mitchell/Mary Jarred/William Herbert/Norman Walker)
10 September Cathedral	Debussy: The blessed damosel (w. Kathleen Ferrier) Dvořák: Te deum (w. Gordon Clinton) Handel: Messiah, Pts 2 and 3 (w. Kathleen Ferrier/ Heddle Nash/Norman Walker)

1949: Hereford

6 September Cathedral	Elgar: The Kingdom (w. Astra Desmond/Eric Greene/Gordon Clinton)
6 September Cathedral	Verdi: Requiem (w. Gladys Ripley/Heddle Nash/ Owen Brannigan)
8 September Cathedral	Dyson: Quo vadis?, Pts 1 and 2†★ (w. Astra Desmond/Heddle Nash/Trevor Anthony)
9 September Shire Hall	A recital (shared with Myra Hess) in which Isobel Baillie sang songs by Arne, Bach, Handel, Parry, Berlioz, Delius, Harty, Gurney, etc.

1950: Gloucester

5 September Cathedral	Haydn: The Creation (w. Eric Greene/Norman Walker)
7 September Cathedral	Howells: Hymnus paradisi†★ (w. William Herbert) Kodály: Missa brevis (w. Gladys Ripley/William Herbert/Norman Walker)
8 September Shire Hall	A concert with the Boyd Neel Orchestra in which Isobel Baillie sang Voi che sapete and Non so più (Mozart: The marriage of Figaro) and Last spring (Grieg)

1951: Worcester

4 September Cathedral	Elgar: The Kingdom (w. Nancy Evans/William Herbert/Harold Williams)
5 September Odeon Theatre	Howells: In greenways★
6 September Cathedral	Howells: Hymnus paradisi★ (w. William Herbert)
7 September Cathedral	Handel: Messiah (w. Mary Jarred/Richard Lewis/ Norman Walker)

1952: Hereford

9 September Cathedral	Haydn: The Creation (w. David Galliver/Richard Standen)
10 September Cathedral	Howells: Hymnus paradisi★ (w. William Herbert)

1953: Gloucester

8 September Cathedral	Mendelssohn: Elijah (w. Gladys Ripley/David Galliver/Bruce Boyce)
11 September Cathedral	Haydn: Coronation Mass Handel: Messiah, Pts 2 and 3 (both w. Nancy Thomas/William Herbert/Norman Walker)

1954: Worcester

6 September Public Hall	A recital (shared with Thomas Matthews) in which Isobel Baillie sang songs by Parry, Berlioz, Delius, Bax and Gurney
7 September Cathedral	Elgar: The Apostles (w. Norma Procter/Wilfred Brown/Gordon Clinton/Norman Walker/ Roderick Jones) Vaughan Williams: Pastoral Symphony★

159

1955: Hereford

7 September Shire Hall	A recital (shared with Julian Bream) in which Isobel Baillie sang songs by Brahms, Sinding, Grieg and Rachmaninov
7 September Cathedral	Handel: Ode for St Cecilia's day (w. William Herbert) G. Bush: In praise of Mary†

---

[1] These 'Four scenes' (The Birth, The Passion, The Gospel and The Faith) were made by H. C. Colles at the request of the Festival Committee for a selection from Messiah which would last approximately one hour.

[2] This was the programme as announced. It was abandoned owing to the outbreak of the Second World War.

Discography of the commercial recordings of Isobel Baillie

THIS discography is divided into three sections: the first a chronological listing of all known sessions, the second a title index, and finally a composer index.

Each session is numbered. Venue and details of accompaniment (where known) are indicated before an examination of each recorded title. The matrix number is the first number to be quoted, with published takes indicated by bold type face (e.g. WAX 4081–**2**). After the relevant musicological details come the UK coupling numbers: column one listing 78 rpm numbers, column two the 45 rpm numbers and column three the LP numbers.

The majority of Isobel Baillie's recordings were sung in English. In this discography the English title has therefore been preferred with the original title in parenthesis. It will be apparent where titles are sung in their original language.

Annotation is given where necessary.

SESSIONS FROM 1924 TO 1974

		Matrix number	Title
Recording for the Gramophone Company			
Session 1	19.2.24 venue unknown[1] piano accompaniment	Bb 4214–1	Sanderson: One morning very early
Recordings for the Columbia Graphophone Company			
Session 2	26.2.26 New Small Room, Petty France piano accompaniment[2]	WA 2959–1 –2	Philips: Among the will<
		WA 2960–1 –2	Cadman: At dawning
Session 3	27.2.26[3] Petty France Hamilton Harty (*piano*)	WT 101	Cadman: At dawning
Session 4	13.10.26 New Small Room, Petty France piano accompaniment	WA 2959–3 –4	Philips: Among the will<
		WA 2960–3 –4	Cadman: At dawning

8 rpm umber	45 rpm number	33⅓ rpm number	Notes
			[1]The location of this recording is not known though it would most probably have been at Hayes, Middlesex. Only one title was recorded (via the acoustic method) and is marked 'test recording'. It was recorded as 'Bella Baillie' as were all recordings made up to and including Session 16.
			[2]It is only presumed that these titles are accompanied by piano. See notes to Session 3.
		RLS 714[4]	[3]The label of this test recording bears the handwritten date 27.2.26 though this could conceivably indicate the date of processing rather than the date of recording. Isobel Baillie remembers that this was her first recording for the Columbia Graphophone Company and that the accompanist for this one matrix was Sir Hamilton Harty. It is almost certain therefore that this session precedes Session 2.
			[4]It is now known that transfer was made a semitone below pitch.

		Matrix number	Title
Session 5	22.2.27 venue unknown orchestral accompaniment	WA 4895-1 -2	Hageman: Do not go my love
		WA 4896-**1** -2	Charles: Do you believe in fairies?
Session 6	23.2.27 venue unknown orchestral accompaniment	WA 4908-**1** -2	Philips: Among the willow
		WA 4909-1 -2	Cadman: At dawning
Session 7	27.2.27[5] venue unknown piano accompaniment	WT 47-1	Sullivan: Orpheus with his lute
		WT 47-2	Cadman: At dawning
Session 8	11.5.27 venue unknown orchestral accompaniment	WAX 2703-1 -2	Handel: Messiah – I know that my Reedemer liveth (1)
		WAX 2704-1 -2	Handel: Messiah – I know that my Reedemer liveth (2)
		WAX 2705-1 -2	Handel: Messiah – He shall feed His flock
Session 9	14.11.27 venue unknown *with Nellie Walker (contralto) orchestral accompaniment	WAX 3113-**1** -2 -3	Offenbach: The tales of Hoffmann – Night of stars and night of love (Barcarolle)*
		WAX 3114-**1** -2	Mozart: The marriage of Figaro – O come do not delay (Deh! vieni non tardar)
		WAX 3115-1 -**2**	Mozart: The marriage of Figaro – You who have knowledge (Voi che sapete)
Session 10	13.9.28 Small Studio, Petty France accompaniment unknown	WA 7809-1 -2 -3	S. Lie: Soft-footed snow (Sne)
		WA 7810-1 -2	Grieg: A dream, Op.48/6 (Ein Traum)
		WAX 4046-1 -2	Schubert: Shepherd on the rock, D.965 (Der Hirt dem Felsen)[6]

'8 rpm number	45 rpm number	33⅓ rpm number	Notes
486		GEMM 217	
486		GEMM 217	

[5]The labels of these test recordings bear the handwritten date 27.2.27. As with Session 3 this may indicate the date of processing rather than that of recording. It is almost certain that Columbia numbered their test recordings (in this instance Western Electric Test – WT) afresh each year.

'8 rpm number	45 rpm number	33⅓ rpm number	Notes
54		GEMM 217	
73		GEMM 217	
73		GEMM 217	

[6]Presumably only the first part of this song was recorded though the recording book does not specify any details save the title.

		Matrix number	Title
Session 11	24.9.28 Small Studio, Petty France Charles Draper (*clarinet*) G. Ison (*piano*)[7]	WAX 4080-**1** -2	Schubert: Shepherd on the rock, D.965 (Der Hirt au' dem Felsen) (1)
		WAX 4081-**1** -2	Schubert: Shepherd on the rock, D.965 (Der Hirt au dem Felsen) (2)
Session 12	3.10.28 Small Studio, Petty France piano accompaniment	WA 7809-4 -5	S. Lie: Soft-footed snow (Sne)
		WA 7810-3 -4	Grieg: A dream Op.48/6 (Ein Traum)
Session 13	9.11.28[8] Large Studio, Petty France ★Ernest Hall (*trumpet*) orchestra/Charles Prentice[9]	WAX 4272-**1** -2	Handel: Samson – Let the bright Seraphim (1)★
		WAX 4273-**1** -2	Handel: Samson – Let the bright Seraphim (2)★
		WAX 4274-**1** -2	Handel: Joshua – Oh! Had Jubal's lyre
Session 14	13.11.28 Large Studio, Petty France orchestral accompaniment	WAX 4275-**1** -2 -3	Handel: Theodora – Angels ever bright and fair
		WA 8095-**1** -2	Mendelssohn: Elijah – Hear ye, Israel (1)
		WA 8096-**1** -2	Mendelssohn: Elijah – Hear ye, Israel (2)
Session 15	27.2.29 Small Studio, Petty France piano accompaniment	WAX 4700-**1** -2 -3	Head: A blackbird singing (No. 3 of 'Over the rim of the moon')
		WAX 4701-**1** -2	Kjerulf: Synnove's song (Synnöves Sang)
Session 16	19.4.29 Large Studio, Petty France Francis Russell (*tenor*) orchestral accompaniment	WAX 4859-**1** -2 -3	Puccini: Madam Butterfly – Give me your darling hands (Dammi ch'io bac
Session 17	[10]7.2.30 Central Hall, Westminster orchestral accompaniment[11]	WAX 5373-**1** -2 -3	Mendelssohn: On wings o' song, Op.34/2 (Auf Flügeln des Gesanges)
		WAX 5374-**1** -2 -3	Bach-Gounod: Ave Maria
Session 18	11.2.30 Central Hall, Westminster orchestral accompaniment[12]	WAX 5377-**1** -2	Offenbach: The tales of Hoffmann – Doll's song
		WAX 5378-**1** -2 -3	Arditi: The dream of hom (Il bacio)

rpm number	45 rpm number	33⅓ rpm number	Notes
13		GEMM 217	[7]This information taken from the recording book. The pianist is uncredited on the record label.
13		GEMM 217	
70		RLS 714 GEMM 217	[8]Booklet to RLS 714 incorrectly states recording date as 4.11.28 for WAX 4272 & WAX 4273.
70		RLS 714 GEMM 217	
7		RLS 714 GEMM 217	[9]Although the Archives indicate Charles Prentice as conductor only for WAX 4274 it is assumed that he also conducted the remaining titles of this session.
7		GEMM 217	
7		GEMM 217	
7		GEMM 217	
4		RLS 714	
			[10]All recordings from this session onwards were made as Isobel Baillie.
			[11]Isobel Baillie recalls Stanford Robinson to be the conductor of this session.
			[12]Isobel Baillie recalls Stanford Robinson to be the conductor of this session.

		Matrix number	Title
Sessions 19–21	Central Hall, Westminster Clara Serena (*contralto*) Parry Jones (*tenor*) Tom Purvis (*tenor*) Harold Williams (*baritone*) BBC National Chorus/ orchestra/Stanford Robinson		Mendelssohn: Elijah (*slight abridged*)
Session 19	25.2.30	WA 10115-1 **-2** -3	No. 21 Hear ye, Israel (1)
		WA 10116-1 **-2** -3	No. 33 Night falleth roune me (*with HW*)
Session 20	26.2.30	WA 10118-**1** -2	No. 21 Hear ye, Israel (2)
		WA 10119-1 **-2** -3	No. 8 What have I to do with thee? (1) (*with HW*)
		WA 10120-1 **-2**	No. 8 What have I to do with thee? (2) (*with HW*)
Session 21	1.3.30	WA 10135-1 **-2**	No. 2 Lord, bow Thine e: to our prayer (*with CS*)
		WA 10144-**1** -2	No. 15 Cast thy burden (*with CS, PJ & HW*)
		WA 10145-1 **-2** -3	No. 35 Above Him stood the Seraphim (*with CS*)
		WA 10178-**1** -2 -3	No. 19 O Lord Thou has overthrown[13] (*with HW*
Session 22	26.3.30 Large Studio, Petty France accompaniment unknown	WAX 5483-1 -2 -3	Bach-Gounod: Ave Maria
		WAX 5484-1 -2	Mendelssohn: On wings (song, Op. 34/2 (Auf Flügeln des Gesanges)
Session 23	29.5.30 Central Hall, Westminster accompaniment unknown	WAX 5591-1 -2 -3	Bach-Gounod: Ave Maria
		WAX 5592-1 -2 -3	Mendelssohn: On wings (song, Op. 34/2 (Auf Flügeln des Gesanges)

8 rpm number	45 rpm number	33⅓ rpm number	Notes
B 58		RLS 714	
B 61			
B 58		RLS 714	
B 52		RLS 714	
B 52		RLS 714	
B 50			[13]Record label states 'the youth' – a role sung by Isobel Baillie.
B 55			
B 1336			
B 62			
B 57			

		Matrix number	Title
Session 24	29.8.30 Central Hall, Westminster accompaniment unknown	WAX 5591-4 -5 -6	Bach-Gounod: Ave Maria
		WAX 5592-4 -5	Mendelssohn: On wings of song, Op.34/2 (Auf Flügeln des Gesanges)
Session 25	18.9.30 Large Studio, Petty France orchestral accompaniment[14]	WAX 5377-3 -4 -5	Offenbach: The tales of Hoffmann – Doll's song
		WAX 5378-4 -5 -6	Arditi: The dream of home (Il bacio)
Session 26	1.10.30 Central Hall, Westminster with cello, harp and organ	WAX 5769-1 -2 -3	Mendelssohn: On wings of song, Op.34/2 (Auf Flügeln des Gesanges)
		WAX 5770-1 -2 -3	Bach-Gounod: Ave Maria
Session 27	13.2.31 Central Hall, Westminster Organ accompaniment	WAX 5970-1 -2 -3	Mascagni: Ave Maria[15]
		WAX 5971-1 -2 -3	Mendelssohn: Psalm 55 – O for the wings of a dove
Session 28	7.7.31 Central Hall, Westminster Clara Serena (*contralto*) Francis Russell (*tenor*) Norman Allin (*bass*) Clarence Raybould (*organ*)	WAX 6163-1 -2	Sacred songs medley (1)[16]
		WAX 6164-1 -2 -3	Sacred songs medley (2)[17]
Session 29	25.1.32 venue unknown Clarence Raybould (*piano*)	CA 12379-1 -2	Schubert: The Trout, D.550 (Die Forelle)[18]
		CA 12380-1 -2	Schubert: Gretchen at the spinning wheel, D. 118 (Gretchen am Spinnrade)
Session 30	9.3.32 venue unknown piano accompaniment	CA 12379-3 -4	Schubert: The Trout, D.550 (Die Forelle)
		CA 12380-3 -4	Schubert: Gretchen at the spinning wheel, D.118 (Gretchen am Spinnrade)

rpm nber	45 rpm number	33⅓ rpm number	Notes
165		GEMM 217	[14]Isobel Baillie recalls Stanford Robinson to be the conductor of this session.
165		GEMM 217	
230	SCD 2113	HQM 1118	
301			
230	SCD 2113		[15]A vocal arrangement of the *Intermezzo* from *Cavalleria Rusticana*.
301			
296			[16]Adams: *The holy city*/Mason: *Nearer my God to Thee*/Liddle: *Abide with me*.
296			[17]Cowen: *The better land*/Allitsen: *The Lord is my light*/Sullivan: *The lost chord*.
836			[18]Recording book states that both titles were intended for the 'Columbia History of Music' but in the event only *Gretchen at the spinning wheel* was used coupled with *Memnon* sung by Harold Williams.

		Matrix number	Title
Session 31	24.3.32 Central Hall, Westminster	CAX 6359-**1** -2	Sacred songs medley (1)[19]
	Catherine Stewart (*contralto*) Heddle Nash (*tenor*) Norman Allin (*bass*) organ, violin & harp	CAX 6360-**1** **-2** -3	Sacred songs medley (2)[20]
Session 32	5.5.32 Petty France piano accompaniment	CA 12380-5 -6	Schubert: Gretchen at the spinning wheel, D.118 (Gretchen am Spinnrade)
		CA 12675-1 -2	Trad.: The flowers of the forest
		CA 12676-1 -2	Trad.: O can ye sew cushions?[21]
Session 33	20.10.32 venue unknown Muriel Brunskill (*contralto*) Heddle Nash (*tenor*)	CA 13155-1 -2 -3	Hedgcock: Sleep, my Saviour, sleep
	Norman Allin (*bass*) & string orchestra	CA 13156-1 -2 -3	Grüber: Silent night, holy night

Recording for the Decca Record Company

Session 34	c.1935 venue unknown chorus/BBC Theatre Orchestra/Stanford	TA 1946-1 -2 **-3**	'On wings of song' – film selection (1)[22]
	Robinson	TA 1947-1 -2	'On wings of song' – film selection (2)[23]

Recording for the Gramophone Company

Session 35	24.5.38 Royal Albert Hall, London Elsie Suddaby (*soprano*) Astra Desmond (*contralto*) chorus and orchestra/Sir Hugh Allen	2EA 5750-**1**	Purcell: To heart-easing mirth[25]

rpm mber	45 rpm number	33⅓ rpm number	Notes
X 373			[19]Wilson: *As pants the hart*/Schubert: *Ave Maria*, D.839/Gounod: *Nazareth*.
X 373			[20]Gounod: *There is a green hill far away*/Bach-Gounod: *Ave Maria*/Mendelssohn: *O for the wings of a dove*.
			[21]with violin obbligato.
B 976	SEG 7615	HQM 1118	
B 976	SEG 7615	HQM 1118	
90			[22]Puccini: *La Bohème – Si mi chiamano Mimì & Quando m'en vo*/Verdi: *Rigoletto – Bella figlia*.
90			[23]Schertzinger: *Love me forever*/Arditi: *Il bacio*/Denza: *Funiculi–Funicula*.
3016			[24]Recorded live at the Empire Day Royal Command Concert.
			[25]This title is an arrangement by Walford Davies of Purcell's *Ah! How pleasant 'tis to love*, Z.353 to new words *Haste thee nymph* from Milton's *L'Allegro*.

	Matrix number	Title

Recordings for the Columbia Graphophone Company

		Matrix number	Title
Session 36	15.10.38 No. 1 Studio, Abbey Road Stiles-Allen, Elsie Suddaby,	CAX 8367–1 –1A –2 **–2A**	Vaughan Williams: Serena to music (1)
	Eva Turner (sopranos), Margaret Balfour, Astra Desmond, Muriel Brunskill, Mary Jarred	CAX 8368–1 –1A –2 **–2A**	Vaughan Williams: Serena to music (2)
	(contraltos), Heddle Nash, Walter Widdop, Parry Jones, Frank Titterton (tenors), Roy Henderson,	CAX 8369–**1** –1A –2	Vaughan Williams: Serena to music (3)
	Harold Williams (baritones) Robert Easton, Norman Allin (basses), BBC Symphony Orchestra/Sir Henry Wood.	CAX 8370–**1** –1A –2 –2A	Vaughan Williams: Serena to music (4)
Session 37	4.6.41 No. 3 Studio, Abbey Road Gerald Moore (piano)	CA 18516–1 –2	Grieg: A dream Op.48/6 (Ein Traum)
		CAX 8859–1 –2 –3	Schubert: Ave Maria, D.8
		CAX 8860–1 –2	Schubert: Gretchen at the spinning wheel, D.118 (Gretchen am Spinnrad
		CA 18517–1 –2	Tchaikovsky: None but t weary heart Op.6/6
Session 38	24.6.41 Civic Hall, Wolverhampton *Anthony Pini (cello) City of Birmingham Orchestra/Basil Cameron	CA 18560–1 –2	J. S. Bach: Cantata No. 2 – Ah! Yes! Just so
		CAX 8871–1 –2 –3 –4 –5 **–6**[26]	Handel: Rodelinda – Art thou troubled?
		CAX 8872–**1** –2	J. S. Bach: Cantata No. 6 My heart ever faithful*
		CAX 8873–**1**	Mozart: La finta giardini – A maiden's is an evil plight

78 rpm number	45 rpm number	33⅓ rpm number	Notes
X 757	SED 5553		
X 757	SED 5553		
X 758	SED 5553		
X 758	SED 5553		
B 2067			[26]Transfers were made of CAX 8871 on 7.7.41 (-3 & -4) and again on 11.7.41 (-5 & -6). The recording book does not state whether -1 or -2 was used for this transfer.
X 1022	SCD 2212	RLS 714	
X 1022	SCD 2212	HQM 1015	
X 1080		HQM 1118	

		Matrix number	Title
Session 39	17.7.41 Kingsway Hall accompaniment unknown	CAX 8880-1 -2 -3	Handel: Messiah – I know that my Reedemer liveth (1)
		CAX 8881-1 -2 -3	Handel: Messiah – I know that my Redeemer liveth (2)
		CAX 8882-1	Purcell: The Blessed Virgin's Expostulation, Z.196 (1)
		CAX 8883-1 -2	Purcell: The Blessed Virgin's Expostulation, Z.196 (2)
Session 40	5.8.41 Kingsway Hall accompaniment unknown	CAX 8880-4 -5	Handel: Messiah – I know that my Reedemer liveth (1)
		CAX 8881-4 -5	Handel: Messiah – I know that my Redeemer livet (2)
	Arnold Goldsborough (organ)	CAX 8882-2 -3 -4	Purcell: The Blessed Virgin's Expostulation, Z.196 (1)
		CAX 8883-3 -4	Purcell: The Blessed Virgin's Expostulation, Z.196 (2)
Session 41	8.8.41 No. 1 Studio, Abbey Road Gerald Moore (*piano*)	CA 18645-1 -2	Grieg: A dream, Op.48/6 (Ein Traum)
		CA 18517-3	Tchaikovsky: None but the weary heart, Op.6/6
		CAX 8860-3 -4	Schubert: Gretchen at the spinning wheel, D.118 (Gretchen am Spinnrade
		CA 18643-1 -2	Schubert: Lullaby D.498 (Wiegenlied)
		CA 18644-1 -2	Schubert: To music D.547 (An die Musik)
Session 42	12.9.41 No. 3 Studio, Abbey Road Gerald Moore (*piano*)	CA 18644-3 -4	Schubert: To music, D.547 (An die Musik)
		CA 18645-3 -4	Grieg: A dream, Op.48/6 (Ein Traum)
		CA 18713-1 -2	Grieg: With a waterlily Op.26/4 (Med en Vandlilje)

rpm number	45 rpm number	33⅓ rpm number	Notes
X 1031		HQM 1015	
X 1031		HQM 1015	
2067		RLS 714	[27]It is not known which take was used for this LP transfer.
		RLS 714[27]	

		Matrix number	Title
Session 43	23.9.41 Belle Vue Gardens, Manchester Hallé Orchestra/Leslie Heward	CAX 8880-**6** -7	Handel: Messiah – I know that my Redeemer livet (1)
		CAX 8881-**6** -7	Handel: Messiah – I know that my Redeemer livet (2)
		CAX 8929-**1** -2	Haydn: The Creation – With verdure clad (1)
		CAX 8930-**1** -2	Haydn: The Creation – With verdure clad (2)
Session 44	19.2.42 No. 3 Studio, Abbey Road Gerald Moore (*piano*)	CA 18924-**1** -2	Purcell: Stript of their gr our groves appear, Z.4
		CA 18925-1 -2	Purcell: I saw that you w grown so high, Z.387
		CA 18926-1 **-2**	Trad. arr. Diack: Ca' yowes to the knowes
		CA 18927-**1** -2	a) Trad.: John Anderson, Jo b) Trad. arr. Stephens: ower young to marry y
Session 45	4.3.42 Houldsworth Hall, Manchester Hallé Orchestra/Leslie Heward	CAX 9002-1 -2 -3 **-4**[28] -5	Haydn: The Seasons – how pleasing to the ser
		CAX 9003-1 -2 -3 **-4**[29]	Purcell: The Fairy Quee Hark! The echoing air
		CAX 9004-1 **-2**	Handel: Solomon – With th'unsheltered moor tread
Session 46	5.6.42 No. 3 Studio, Abbey Road Gerald Moore (*piano*)	CA 18999-1 -2 -3 -4 -5	Scott: Think on me
		CA 19000-1 -2	Trad.: Comin' through t rye

rpm mber	45 rpm number	33⅓ rpm number	Notes
X 1036	SCD 2081 SEG 7755	HQM 1015	
X 1036	SCD 2081 SEG 7755	HQM 1015	
X 1052		HQM 1015	
X 1052		HQM 1015	
B 2093		RLS 714	
B 2076			
B 2076			
X 1234			[28]Transfers were made of CAX 9002 on 5.2.46 (-3 & -4) and again on 25.2.46 (-5). The recording book does not state whether -1 or -2 was used for this transfer.
X 1234		HQM 1118	[29]Transfers were made of CAX 9003 on 5.2.46 (-4) but the recording book does not state which of the earlier takes was used for this transfer.
X 1080		HQM 1118	

		Matrix number	*Title*
Session 47	18.6.42 No. 3 Studio, Abbey Road Gerald Moore (*piano*)	CA 18924-3 -4	Purcell: Stript of their gre our groves appear, Z. 4
		CA 19001-**1** -2	Trad.: arr. Lees: O can ye sew cushions?
		CA 18713-3 -4	Grieg: With a waterlily, Op.26/4 (Med en Vandlilje)
		CA 18999-6 **-7**	Scott: Think on me
		CA 19000-3 **-4**	Trad.: Comin' through th rye
Session 48	8.9.42 No. 3 Studio, Abbey Road Gerald Moore (*piano*)	CA 18925-**3** -4	Purcell: I saw that you we grown so high, Z. 387
		CA 19061-1 -2	Arne: The judgement of Paris – O ravishing delight
Session 49	21.9.42 No. 3 Studio, Abbey Road Gerald Moore (*piano*)	CA 19061-**3**	Arne: The judgement of Paris – O ravishing delight
		CA 19064-1 -2	Trad. arr. Dolmetsch: Ha you seen but a whyte li grow?
Session 50	11.11.42 Abbey Road Studios[31] John Francis, A. Hedges (*flutes*), John Moore (*cello*), Gerald Moore (*piano*)	CAX 9060-1 **-2** -3 -4	J. S. Bach: Cantata No. 2 – Shall pales be the last. . .Flocks in pasture (1)
		CAX 9061-1 **-2** -3 -4	J. S. Bach: Cantata No. 2 – Flocks in pastures (2)
Session 51	18.3.43 Houldsworth Hall, Manchester Arthur Lockwood (*trumpet*) Hallé Orchestra/Warwick Braithwaite	CAX 9070-**1** -2	Handel: Samson – Let the bright Seraphim (1)
		CAX 9071-**1** -2 -3	Handel: Samson – Let the bright Seraphim (2)
Session 52	2.4.43 No. 3 Studio, Abbey Road Gerald Moore (*piano*)	CA 19215-1 -2	Arne: Where the bee suc
		CA 19216-**1** -2	Trad. arr. Diack: O whis an' I'll come to you
		CA 19217-**1**	Trad.: Annie Laurie

rpm number	45 rpm number	33⅓ rpm number	Notes
B 2111			
B 2080		HQM 1118	
B 2080		HQM 1118	
B 2093			
B 2121		RLS 714	[30]It is not known which take was used for this LP transfer.
		RLS 714[30]	
X 1103	SCD 2135 SED 5557		[31]Takes -1 and -2 of each matrix were recorded in No. 1 Studio whilst takes -3 and -4 were recorded in No. 3 Studio.
X 1103	SCD 2135 SED 5557		
X 1113	SEG 7755	HQM 1015	
X 1113	SEG 7755	HQM 1015	
			[32]Recording date incorrectly quoted in booklet as 8.4.43.
B 2111		HQM 1118	
		RLS 714[32]	

		Matrix number	Title
Session 53	3.8.43 No. 3 Studio, Abbey Road Gerald Moore (*piano*)	CA 19297-**1** -**2** -**3**	Brahms: Sister dear, DV.1 (Schwesterlein, Schwesterlein)
		CA 19298-**1** -**2**	Grieg: With a waterlily, Op.26/4 (Med en Vandlilje)
Session 54	2.9.43 No. 3 Studio, Abbey Road Gerald Moore (*piano*)	CA 19317-**1** -**2**	Rachmaninov: a) Lilacs Op.21/5 b) Before my window, Op.26/10
		CA 19215-**3** -**4**	Arne: Where the bee suck
Session 55	15.10.43 Kingsway Hall Bertram Harrison (*organ*)	CAX 9118-**1** -**2**	J. S. Bach: a) In faith I qu wait, BWV. 466 (Ich h treulich still) b) Come sweetest death, BWV. 478 (Komm, süsser Tod)
		CAX 9119-**1** -**2**	Attr. Stölzel[33]: Be Thou with me (Bist du bei m
Session 56	26.1.44 No. 3 Studio, Abbey Road Gerald Moore (*piano*)	CA 19417-**1** -**2**	Trad. German arr. Morri Alleluia (A joyous East Hymn) (Let joyful prai to heaven ascend)
		CA 19418-**1** -**2**	Trad. French arr. Hazelhurst: O leave yo sheep (Quittez pasteurs
		CA 19419-**1** -**2**	Delius: Love's philosophy
Session 57	27.1.44 No. 3 Studio, Abbey Road Gerald Moore (*piano*)	CA 19420-**1** -**2**	Delius: Twilight fancies
		CA 19421-**1** -**2**	Harty: Lane o' the thrush
		CA 19422-**1** -**2**	Quilter: To daisies Op.8/ (from 'To Julia')
Session 58	21.3.44 Liverpool Philharmonic Hall Liverpool Philharmonic Orchestra/ Sir Malcolm Sargent	CAX 9167-**1** -**2** -**3**	Handel: Acis and Galatea O didst thou know. . . when the dove (1)
		CAX 9168-**1** -**2**	Handel: Acis and Galatea As when the dove (2)
		CAX 9169-**1** -**2**	Handel: Messiah – Rejoic greatly
		CAX 9170-**1** -**2**	Handel: Messiah – If God for us

8 rpm number	45 rpm number	33¹⁄₃ rpm number	Notes
·B 2120		RLS 714	
·B 2120		RLS 714	
·B 2303		HQM 1118	
·B 2121		RLS 714	
·X 1133			[33]*Bist du bei mir* appears in the Clavierbüchlein für Anna Magdelena Bach (1725) and Schmeider catalogues it as BWV. 508. It is now generally considered however to have been composed by Gottfried Heinrich Stölzel (1690–1745).
X 1133			
B 2135			
B 2135			
B 2303			
X 1158		HQM 1118	
X 1158		HQM 1118	
X 1154		RLS 714	
X 1154		RLS 714	

		Matrix number	Title
Session 59[34] 27.2.45	No. 1 Studio, Abbey Road London Symphony Orchestra/ Maurice Miles	CAX 9218-1 -2	Haydn: The Creation – And God said. . .On mighty pens (1)
		CAX 9223-1 -2	Haydn: The Creation – On mighty pens (2)
		CAX 9251-1 -2	Handel: Judas Maccabaeus O let eternal honours. . .From mighty kings (1)
Session 60 7.3.45	No. 1 Studio, Abbey Road London Symphony Orchestra/ Maurice Miles	CAX 9256-1 -2	Handel: Judas Maccabaeus From mighty kings (2)
		CAX 9257-1 -2	Handel: Messiah – How beautiful are the feet
		CAX 9258-1 -2	Handel: Judas Maccabaeus O grant it heaven. . .So shall the lute and harp awake
Session 61 31.5.45	No. 3 Studio, Abbey Road Gerald Moore (*piano*)	CA 19419-**3**	Delius: Love's philosophy
		CA 19420-**3** -**4**	Delius: Twilight fancies
		CA 19421-**3**	Harty: Lane o' the thrushes

Recording for the Gramophone Company

		Matrix number	Title
Session 62 4.7.45	No. 1 Studio, Abbey Road Joan Hammond (*soprano*) Joan Fullerton (*soprano*) Dennis Noble (*baritone*) chorus/Philharmonia String Orchestra/Constant Lambert (with Boris Ord, *harpsichord*)		Purcell: Dido and Aeneas[35] (*complete*)
		2EA 10521-**1** -2 -3	No. 7 See your royal guest appears (*with JH & DN*) No. 10 Pursue thy conquest love
		2EA 10526-**1** -2 -3	No. 26 Haste, haste to town (*with JH & DN*)
		2EA 10529-1 -**2** -3	No. 33 Your counsel, all is urg'd in vain
		2EA 10525-1 -**2**	No. 23 Thanks to these lonesome vales No. 24 Oft she visits this loved mountain[36]
		2EA 10518-1 -**2**	No. 1 Shake the cloud from off your brow
		2EA 10519-1 -**2**	No. 3 Grief increases by concealing (*with JF*)
		2EA 10520-**1** -2 -3	No. 5 Whence could so much virtue spring? (*with JH*) No. 6 Fear no danger to ensue

8 rpm mber	45 rpm number	33¹⁄₃ rpm number	Notes
			[34]There is no significance to be drawn from the random allocation of matrix numbers.
B 2178		HQM 1118	
B 2178		HQM 1118	
			[35]Edited by E. J. Dent
3472 7631			[36]No. 24 assigned in score to the Second Woman but here sung by Isobel Baillie in the role of Belinda.
3475 7633			
3476 7630			
3474 7634			
3471 7628			
3471 7629			
3472 7630			

	Matrix number	Title

Recordings for the Columbia Graphophone Company

		Matrix number	Title
Session 63	21.9.45 No. 3 Studio, Abbey Road	CA 19861-1 -2	Purcell: Come ye sons of a – Sound the trumpet
	Kathleen Ferrier (*contralto*) Gerald Moore (*piano*)	CA 19862-1 -2	Purcell: a) The Indian Queen – Let us wander b) King Arthur – Shepher cease decoying
		CA 19863-1	Mendelssohn: I would that my love Op. 63/1 (Ich wollt' meine Liebe ergösse sich)
		CA 19864-1 -2	Mendelssohn: Greeting Op.63/3 (Gruss)
		CA 19865-1	Trad.: O wert thou in the cauld blast?
		CA 19866-1 -2	Trad.: Scottish: Turn ye t me
Session 64	17.1.46 Kingsway Hall, London	CAX 9432-1 -2	Handel: Messiah – How beautiful are the feet
	Philharmonia Orchestra/ Reginald Jacques	CAX 9433-1 -2	Handel: Messiah – Come unto Him
		CAX 9434-1 -2	Haydn: The Creation – O mighty pens (1)
		CAX 9435-1 -2	Haydn: The Creation – O mighty pens (2)
Session 65	18.1.46 Kingsway Hall, London ★Herbert Dawson (*organ*)	CAX 9439-1 -2	Handel: Judas Maccabaeus O grant it heaven. . .S shall the lute and harp
	Philharmonia Orchestra/ Reginald Jacques	CAX 9440-1 -2	Mozart: Exsultate jubilate K. 165 (1)★
		CAX 9441-1 -2	Mozart: Exsultate jubilate K. 165 (2)★
		CAX 9442-1 -2	Mozart: Exsultate jubilate K. 165 (3)★
Session 66	19.6.46 (am) Kingsway Hall, London	CAX 9560-1 -2	Haydn: The Creation – C mighty pens (1)
	Philharmonia Orchestra/ George Weldon	CAX 9561-1 -2	Haydn: The Creation – C mighty pens (2)
		CAX 9562-1 -2	Handel: Judas Maccabaeu From mighty kings (1)

8 rpm number	45 rpm number	33⅓ rpm number	Notes
B 2201	SED 5530	HLM 7002	
B 2201	SED 5530	HLM 7002	
B 2194	SED 5526	HLM 7002	
B 2194	SED 5526	HQM 1072 HLM 7002	
		RLS 714[37]	[37]It is not known which take was used for this LP transfer.
X 1392		RLS 714	
X 1392		RLS 714	

		Matrix number	Title
Session 67	19.6.46 (pm) No. 1 Studio, Abbey Road Harry Mortimer (*trumpet*) Ernest Lush (*harpsichord*) Philharmonia Orchestra/ George Weldon	CAX 9566[38]-1 -2	J. S. Bach: Cantata No. 51 Allelujah
Session 68	19.8.46 No. 3 Studio, Abbey Road Gerald Moore (*piano*)	CA 20154-**1** -2	Trad. Celtic arr. Kennedy-Fraser: Kishmul's galley
		CA 20155-**1** -2	Trad. Celtic arr. Kennedy-Fraser: A fairy's love son
		CA 21056-**1** -2	Trad. Celtic arr. Kennedy-Fraser: An Eriskay love lilt
		CA 21057-**1** -2	Trad. Celtic arr. Lawson & Moore: Skye boat song
Session 69	26.9.46 Huddersfield Town Hall Liverpool Philharmonic Orchestra/Sir Malcolm Sargent		Handel: Messiah (*complete*)
		CAX 9604-**1** -2 -3	No. 18 Rejoice greatly
		CAX 9605-**1** -2	No. 20 Come unto Him
		CAX 9606-**1** -2 -3	No. 45 I know that my Redeemer liveth (1)
		CAX 9607-**1** -2	No. 45 I know that my Redeemer liveth (2)
		CAX 9608-**1** -2 -3	Nos. 14–16 There were shepherds. . .And lo, th angel of the Lord. . .An suddenly
		CAX 9609-**1** -2 -3	No. 38 How beautiful are the feet

188

'8 rpm number	45 rpm number	33⅓ rpm number	Notes
			[38]Matrices CAX 9563 to CAX 9565 inclusive are Haydn's *Trumpet Concerto* played by Harry Mortimer with above orchestra and conductor.
⟩B 2277			
⟩B 2239			
⟩B 2239		HQM 1118	
⟩B 2277			
⟩X 1290 ⟩X 8224			
⟩X 1291 ⟩X 8231			
⟩X 1299 ⟩X 8239		RLS 714	
⟩X 1299 ⟩X 8240		RLS 714	
⟩X 1289 ⟩X 8225			
⟩X 1296 ⟩X 8235		RLS 714	

	Matrix number	Title
Recordings for the Gramophone Company		
Session 70[39] 8.4.47 No. 3 Studio, Abbey Road Margaret Field-Hyde (*soprano*), Gladys Winmill (*mezzo-soprano*) René Soames (*tenor*), Keith Falkner (*baritone*)/Boris Ord	2EA 11820-**1** -2	a) Wilbye: Flora gave me fairest flowers b) Vautor: Sweet Suffolk owl
	2EA 11821-**1** -2 -3	a) Gibbons: Dainty fine bir‹ b) Weelkes: Lady the birds right fairly
	2EA 11822-**1** -2 -3	Pilkington: Care for thy soul
Gladys Winmill (*mezzo-soprano*), René Soames (*tenor*), Keith Falkner (*baritone*)/Boris Ord	2EA 11823-**1** -2 -3	Farmer: Fair Phyllis I saw
Session 71 9.4.47 No. 3 Studio, Abbey Road Gladys Winmill (*mezzo-soprano*), René Soames (*tenor*), Keith Falkner (*baritone*)/Boris Ord	2EA 11824-**1** -2	Morley ed. Fellowes: Now is the gentle season
Recordings for the Columbia Graphophone Company		
Sessions 72–75 Huddersfield Town Hall Gladys Ripley (*contralto*) James Johnston (*tenor*) Harold Williams (*baritone*) Huddersfield Choral Society/Liverpool Philharmonic Orchestra/ Sir Malcolm Sargent		Mendelssohn: Elijah (*slightl‹ abridged*)
Session 72 29.5.47	CAX 9920-**1** -2	No. 21 Hear ye Israel
	CAX 9921-**1** -2	No. 8 What have I to do with thee? (1) (*with HW*)
	CAX 9922-**1** -2 -3	No. 8 What I have to do with thee? (2) (*with HW*)
	CAX 9924-**1** -2	No. 19 O Lord thou hast overthrown (*with HW*)

78 rpm number	45 rpm number	33¹₃ rpm number	Notes
C 3748			[39]All items edited by E. H. Fellowes.
C 3748			
C 3749			
C 3749			
C 3750			
DX 1416 DX 8289		RLS 730	
DX 1411 DX 8286		RLS 730	
DX 1411 DX 8287		RLS 730	
DX 1415 DX 8280		RLS 730	

		Matrix number	Title
Session 73	30.5.47 (am)	CAX 9925-1 -2	No. 33 Night falleth round me (*with HW*)
Session 74	30.5.47 (pm)	CAX 9931-1 -2	No. 15 Cast thy burden (*with GR, JJ & HW*)
		CAX 9932-1 -2	No. 2 Lord, bow Thine ear (*with GR*)
Session 75	2.6.47	CAX 9949-1 -2	No. 41 O come everyone that thirsteth (*with GR, JJ & HW*)
		CAX 9951-1 -2	No. 41 O come everyone that thirsteth[40] (*with GR, JJ & HW*)
Session 76	27.8.47 Kingsway Hall, London Philharmonia Orchestra/ Sir Malcolm Sargent	CAX 9988-1 -2	Dyson: The Canterbury Pilgrims – A good wife was there beside Bath
		CAX 10002-1 -2	Dvořák: The spectre's bride – Where art thou, father dear? (1)
		CAX 10003-1 -2	Dvořák: The spectre's bride – Where art thou, father dear? (2)
Session 77	28.8.47 Kingsway Hall, London Philharmonia Orchestra/ Sir Malcolm Sargent	CAX 10004-1 -2	Elgar: The Kingdom – The sun goeth down (1)
		CAX 10005-1 -2	Elgar: The Kingdom – The sun goeth down (2)
		CAX 10003-3	Dvořák: The spectre's bride – Where art thou, father dear? (2)
Session 78	16.9.47 No. 1 Studio, Abbey Road Philharmonia Orchestra/ Walter Susskind	CA 20494-1 -2	Mozart: The marriage of Figaro – Still Susanna delays. . .Vanish'd are ye (1) (E Susanna non vien. . .Dove sono)
		CA 20495-1 -2	Mozart: The marriage of Figaro – Vanish'd are ye (2) (Dove sono)
		CAX 10034-1 -2	Mozart: The marriage of Figaro – Thou, o love (Porgi amor)
		CAX 10035-1	Grieg: Spring, Op.33/2 (Våren)

78 rpm number	45 rpm number	33⅓ rpm number	Notes
)X 1420)X 8294		RLS 730	
)X 1414)X 8283		RLS 730	
)X 1409)X 8282		RLS 730	
)X 1423)X 8289		RLS 730	[40]A transfer of CAX 9949-1 with no 'rill out'.
		HQM 1015[41]	[41]It is not known which take was used for this LP transfer. Sleeve of HQM 1015 inaccurately quotes recording date as 5.2.48.
)X 1471		HQM 1118	
)X 1471		HQM 1118	
)X 1443		HQM 1015	
)X 1443		HQM 1015	
)B 2444			
)B 2444			

		Matrix number	Title
Session 79	28.10.47 No. 1 Studio, Abbey Road	CA 20556-1 -2	Trad: O come all ye faithfu
	Gladys Ripley (*contralto*) John McHugh (*tenor*)	CA 20557-1 -2	Kirkpatrick arr. Chambers: Away in a manger
	Harold Williams (*baritone*)[42] Herbert Dawson (*organ*)	CA 20558-1 -2	Trad. harmonised Stainer: The Coventry carol
		CA 20559-1 -2	Trad.: The first nowell
Session 80	28.9.48 No. 1 Studio, Abbey Road	CA 20907-1 -2	Holst: Lullay my liking
	★with Herbert Dawson (*organ*)	CA 20908-1 -2	Trad. arr Rooper: Tryste noel
	Gladys Ripley (*contralto*) John McHugh (*tenor*)	CA 20909-1 -2	Trad. arr Wainwright: Christians awake!★
	Harold Williams (*baritone*)[43]	CA 20910-1 -2	Mendelssohn: Hark! The herald angels sing★
Session 81	13.12.48 No. 3 Studio, Abbey Road Gerald Moore (*piano*)	CA 20962-1 -2	Hahn: If my songs were only winged (Si mes ver avaient des ailes)
		CA 20963-1 -2	German: Charming Chloë
		CA 20964-1 -2	Diack: Wee Willie Winkie
		CA 20965-1 -2	Diack: a) Creep afore ye gang b) Feetikins
Session 82	14.2.49 Kingsway Hall, London London Symphony Orchestra/Sir Malcolm Sargent	CAX 10446-1 -2	Handel orch. Wood: Judas Maccabaeus – O let eternal honours. . .From mighty kings (1)
		CAX 10447-1 -2	Handel orch. Wood: Judas Maccabaeus – From mighty kings (2)
		CAX 10448-1	Handel orch. Wood: Alessandro – Ne' trionfa d'Alessandro. . .Lusingh più care (1)
		CAX 10449-1 -2	Handel orch. Wood: Alessandro – Lusinghe più care (2)

78 rpm number	45 rpm number	33⅓ rpm number	Notes
DB 2359	SEG 7615		[42]Singers collectively entitled 'The Celebrity Quartette' on record labels.
DB 2360	SEG 7615		
DB 2360			
DB 2359			
DB 2464			[43]Singers collectively entitled 'The Celebrity Quartette' on record labels.
DB 2465			
DB 2465			
DB 2464			
DB 2489			
DB 2489		HQM 1118	
DB 2662			
DB 2662			
DX 1559	SED 5557	HQM 1015	[44]It is not known which take was used for this LP transfer. The sleeve to HLM 7033 inaccurately states recording date to be 16.2.49.
DX 1559	SED 5557	HQM 1015	
		HLM 7033	
		HLM 7033[44]	

		Matrix number	Title
Session 83[45] 27.2.50 No. 3 Studio, Abbey Road Gerald Moore (*piano*)		CA 21390-**1** -2	Schubert: The brook, D.795/2 (Wohin?)
		CA 21391-1 -2	Schubert: Vital spark of heavenly flame, D.59 (Verklärung)
Session 84 5.7.51 No. 3 Studio, Abbey Road Gerald Moore (*piano*)		CA 21815-1 -2	Schumann: a) The snowdrop, Op.79/26 (Schneeglöckchen) b) Ladybird Op.79/14 (Marienwürmchen)
		CA 21391-4[47] -5 -6	Schubert: Vital spark of heavenly flame D.59 (Verklärung)

Recording for the Decca Record Company

Session 85 December 1953 Kingsway Hall, London John Cameron (*baritone*) London Philharmonic Choir/London Philharmonic Orchestra/ Sir Adrian Boult			Vaughan Williams: A Sea Symphony

Recordings for EMI Records Limited

Session 86 14.8.74 No. 1 Studio, Abbey Road Ivor Newton (*piano*)			Trad.: I will walk with my love Scott: Blackbird's song Harty: The stranger's grave Harty: Grace for light Schubert: The trout, D.550 (Die Forelle) Mendelssohn: St Paul – Jerusalem

78 rpm number	45 rpm number	33⅓ rpm number	Notes
OB 2999		RLS 714	[45]This session also recorded on tape (Reel 1497).
		RLS 714[46]	[46]It is not known which take was used for this LP transfer.
			[47]There is no documentation of CA 21391-3 for either this session or Session 83.
OB 2999			
		LXT 2907/8 ACL 247/8 ECS 583	
		RLS 714	
		RLS 714 RLS 714 RLS 714 HLM 7093	

TITLE INDEX

Numbers are those of sessions.

COMPOSER INDEX

Numbers are those of sessions.

Serenade to music 36
VAUTOR: Sweet Suffolk owl 70
VERDI: Rigoletto 34

WEELKES: Lady, the birds right fairly 70
WILBYE: Flora gave me fairest flowers 70
WILSON: As pants the hart 31

POSTSCRIPT

Since the completion of the discography EMI Records have announced a two-record set (RLS 7703) also entitled 'Never sing louder than lovely.' The following items are included:

PURCELL: The Blessed Virgin's expostulation   Session 40 CAX 8882–2 & 8883–3
Stript of their green our groves appear   Session 44 CA 18924–1
The Fairy Queen – Hark! The echoing air   Session 45 CAX 9003–4
ARNE: The judgement of Paris – O ravishing delight   Session 49 CA 19061–3
Where the bee sucks   Session 54 CA 19215–3
BACH: Cantata No. 208 – Shall pales be the last. . .Flocks in pastures   Session 50 CAX 9060–2 & 9061–2
Cantata No. 68 – My heart ever faithful   Session 38 CAX 8872–1
HANDEL: Acis and Galatea – O didst thou know. . .As when the dove   Session 58 CAX 9167–1 & 9168–2
Messiah – Rejoice greatly   Session 58 CAX 9169–2
Messiah – How beautiful are the feet   Session 69 CAX 9609–1
Messiah – I know that my Redeemer liveth   Session 69 CAX 9606–1 & 9607–1
Messiah – If God be for us   Session 58 CAX 9170–2
Samson – Let the bright Seraphim   Session 51 CAX 9070–1 & 9071–1
Judas Maccabaeus – O let eternal honours. . .From mighty kings   Session 82 CAX 10446–2 & 10447–2
Joshua – O had I Jubal's lyre   Session 13 WAX 4274–2
HAYDN: The Creation – With verdure clad   Session 43 CAX 8929–1 & 8930–1
The Creation – On mighty pens   Session 66 CAX 9560–1 & 9561–2
SANDERSON: One morning very early   Session 1 Bb 4214–1
CADMAN: At dawning   Session 3 WT 101
KJERULF: Synnove's song   Session 15 WAX 4701–2
OFFENBACH: The tales of Hoffman – Doll's song   Session 25 WAX 5377–3
MENDELSSOHN: On wings of song   Session 26 WAX 5769–2
TRAD: O can ye sew cushions?   Session 32 CA 12676–1
TRAD: Comin' through the rye   Session 47 CA 19000–4
TRAD. ARR DIACK: O whistle an' I'll come to you   Session 52 CA 19216–1
DELIUS: Twilight fancies   Session 61 CA 19420–4
TRAD: I will walk with my love   Session 86 RLS 714

Derek Lewis and Bryan Crimp
London, 1982

General Index

205